BUSINESS TO BUSINESS GUIDES

RUSSIAN

BUSINESS TO BUSINESS GUIDES

RUSSIAN

BY

CHARLES BERLITZ

A Perigee Book

Perigee Books
are published by
The Putnam Publishing Group
200 Madison Avenue
New York, NY 10016

Library of Congress Cataloging-in-Publication Data

Berlitz, Charles, date.
  Business to business in Russian / by Charles Berlitz — 1st Perigee ed.
  p. cm.
  ISBN: 0-399-51831-2

1. Russia (Federation) — Guidebooks. 2 Business travel — Russia (Federation)
— Guidebooks. 3. Russian language — Conversation and phrase books. I. Title.
DK510.22.B47   1994   93-27342 CIP
914.704'86—dc20

Cover design by Bob Silverman, Inc.

Printed in the United States of America
1 2 3 4 5 6 7 8 9 10

CONTENTS

HISTORY

1

The history of Russia is the story of contradictory questions. Was Russia part of Europe or part of Asia? Did its Christianity make it part of the West or did its Orthodox church make it a nation of the East? Who would predominate? – those dedicated to creating a uniquely Russian culture or the partisans of the West who wanted to follow Europe's lead in politics, art, and economic development? The tensions between Europe and Asia, East and West, insularity and cosmopolitanism, have shaped Russian history almost from its inception, and continue to form the Russian experience today.

THE GREAT RUSSIAN EMPIRE

Russia's modern history begins in 1682 with the accession of Tsar Peter the Great. One of Peter's most significant acts was the establishment of St. Petersburg instead of, as hitherto, Moscow, as Russia's capital, symbolizing his desire to look towards the West for the model of modernizing Russia.

When Peter I came to power, Russia was still relatively isolated from Europe and the West. Peter's expansion of the Russian Empire to include access to the Baltic Sea changed the geopolitical face of the nation and provided access for the new city of St. Petersburg, window to the West. Peter's modernizing plan included symbolic actions, such as forcing his court to give up Eastern robes in favor of modern Western dress, as well as political moves, such as subjugating the Church to the power of the state. He is also known for building a navy – now that Russia had a coastline – and for modernizing the Russian army.

Another expansion of Russia's power was achieved by Catherine the Great, the German-born wife of Peter III. Under Catherine, the Crimea was annexed in 1783, giving Russia a southern as well as a western coast.

Over the 300 years of the Romanov Empire, Russia's borders expanded to include huge new chunks of both Europe and Asia. In the 17th century, Eastern Siberia was annexed to the growing nation. In the 18th century, Russia took over the Baltic, the Western Ukraine and most of Poland. In the 19th century, Finland, Central Asia, and the Caucasus became part of the Russian empire.

This empire's power was firmly established in 1812, when Napoleon's invading army was routed by the bitter Russian winter – and by the determined Russian army, under the leadership of Kutuzov.

As the empire's military and political power grew, so did its artistic achievements. On both the political and the cultural fronts, Russia maintained its troubled but durable connection with Western Europe.

Since the 18th century, the language of the aristocracy in Russia had been French. Thus, as it entered the 19th century, Russia had no "high culture" in its own language. This situation was changed by the poet Alexander Pushkin, a child of the aristocracy whose poetry was based on the Russian folk tales and fairy tales told to him by his nurse. Pushkin's work won a new respect for the underdeveloped Russia in Europe and created the ongoing debate between the Slavophiles and the Westernizers.

Travelers familiar with Russia will recognize the legacy of this debate even today. Although ostensibly this debate took place primarily among intellectuals and focused on artistic issues, it had – and continues to have – serious political ramifications of concern to all classes. The Slavophiles rejected Western influences, calling for a true Russian national culture based on the spiritual heritage of the Russian Orthodox Church. The Westernizers called for a speedy imitation of Western models. In literary circles, the writer Turgenev became a symbol of the Westernizers, while Dostoevsky represented Slavophile thought. Years later, political analysts would remark that the political figure of Trotsky stood for Westernization – the cosmopolitan connection of Russia to the revolutionary movements of Europe – whereas Stalin represented the Russian tendency to claim a unique and separate heritage isolated from the corrupting influences of the West. Today, fledgling groups like *Pamyat* – "Memory" – call upon the Slavophile traditions of Russian isolationism and religious orthodoxy, whereas Boris Yeltsin's ties to the United States and Europe are seen as the high tide of Westernizing influences.

THE REVOLUTIONARY TRADITION

To some extent, the revolutionary impetus in Russia came from the Western ideals of "liberty, equality, and fraternity", first propounded by the French Revolution and carried into Russia by the officers who fought the French during the Napoleonic Wars. These officers led a revolt in 1825 against the new tsar, Nicholas I, as he took power upon the death of Alexander I. Some 3,000 troops rose up in protest – and were fired on by Nicholas's loyal soldiers. The leaders of this uprising, known as the Decembrists, were hanged for treason, setting the

Russian pattern of revolt and repression.

One of the major issues in the Russia of this period was the condition of the serfs. Russian peasants did not enjoy the legal freedom to leave their holdings, nor the economic freedom to control the products of their labor. Rather, they lived under medieval conditions, bound to the land where they were born and to the landowner who owned that land.

The serfs' lack of freedom was seen as a political scandal, one that flew in the face of "liberty, equality" and the "inalienable rights of man." But it was also seen as an economic issue, a medieval relic that was holding back Russia's entrance into the modern era. When the serfs were finally freed in 1861 under Alexander II, many believed that Russia would experience a surge of economic improvement.

In fact, the ex-serfs remained poor, politically disenfranchised, and virtually illiterate. The Populist Movement – which sent 2,000 adherents into the countryside to organize peasant revolt – was soon followed by Narodnaya Volya, "The People's Will," an underground terrorist organization.

In 1881, The People's Will managed to assassinate the tsar. But far from ending tsarism, this terrorist activity only made it more repressive. This failure caused many Russian revolutionaries to turn to Marxism. Throughout the 19th Century, the new philosophy of Marxism was taking hold in Western Europe. Marxism held that the working class was the major revolutionary force in the modern period, able to change the nature of society through disciplined and united action. During this period, many European Marxist parties believed that the working class could seize power peacefully, winning economic strength through the trade union movement and taking political power through electoral action.

However, this type of politics depended on an educated industrial working class, which was for the most part absent from Russia, still a country of peasants. The European Marxism of the period also relied upon a political system in which free electoral activity was possible – unlike the repressive tsarist monarchy of Russia. As in the similarly underdeveloped and repressive monarchy of Spain, terrorism and anarchism were far more popular political movements in Russia than the disciplined and sophisticated Marxism of Western Europe.

Both in Europe and in Russia, some party activists were beginning to express dissatisfaction with the slow pace of electoral change.

Many began to believe that true social transformation would never take place in that way, and that more radical action was needed. In 1903, the Russian party split into two wings: the Menshevik or "minority" wing, which believed in peaceful and electoral change, and the Bolshevik "majority", led by Lenin, which believed in a centralized party led by full-time revolutionaries.

TWO REVOLUTIONS

Soon after the Russian party split, in 1905, workers marched to petition Tsar Nicholas II for better conditions. The day they marched became known as "Bloody Sunday", because Nicholas ordered his troops to fire upon the unarmed crowd. The Russian people, already demoralized by their loss of the Russo-Japanese War, were further outraged at the Tsar's response. They engaged in a wave of strikes and protests that seemed to be leading to a general strike – a nationwide work stoppage that would have united all the workers of Russia. Fearing such widespread activity, the Tsar backed down. He established the first democratic institution in Russia – the parliament, or duma.

Despite the duma, however, little changed politically or economically in Russia after 1905. Various Marxist, anarchist, and other political parties continued to organize and agitate for change, but with few apparent results.

Then, in 1914, a war began that soon spread across the entire face of Europe. Russia's involvement in this war, on the side of France, Britain, and eventually, the United States, brought destruction and devastation to the troubled nation. As the war took its toll, discontent increased among peasants and workers, and the strength of the revolutionary parties grew. Finally, in February 1917, people rioted for bread in the streets of St. Petersburg. The result of the political upheaval was that Nicholas II abdicated the throne – and ended the tsarist system. Alexander Kerensky came to power as head of Russia's first democratic government – the so-called Provisional Government.

But the change offered by Kerensky was seen by many Russians as too little, too late. Despite the promises of political reform, the peasants in the countryside still clamored in vain for land and bread, while workers in the city continued to experience wartime shortages. Kerensky refused to surrender or withdraw from the war, creating both political and economic problems. Revolutionary movements of all types continued their agitation – leading to the "October Revolution" of 1917, in which the Bolsheviks, led by Lenin, seized power through the soviets (revolutionary councils) of Petrograd (St. Petersburg) and Moscow. (Because Russia at that time followed another calendar, it placed the revolution in October, whereas according to the more modern calendar it later adopted, the revolution took place in November.)

THE EARLY DAYS OF COMMUNISM

The new regime faced what seemed like insurmountable problems at first. The Bolshevik Revolution provoked a counterrevolution. Army officers loyal to the tsar led troops against the Bolsheviks, with the support of the United States, Britain, France, and Japan, each of whom sent troops to intervene in Soviet affairs. Not until 1921 did the Soviet Red Army finally declare victory and allow the new government to preside over a nation in peace.

But World War I and the Civil War had left the Soviet Union in economic disarray. Even as the nation expanded – with the former colonies of the Great Russian Empire joining Russia in a union of autonomous Soviet republics – its problems grew.

During the Civil War, Lenin had presided over an economic structure known as "war communism" – the emergency collectivization of all industries. After the Revolution, many of the country's managers and engineers had emigrated, unwilling to live under the new socialist system. In their absence, the often unskilled and near-illiterate workers had to run the factories themselves, with sometimes impressive results. The emergency arrangements could not be expected to last over time, however, and in 1921 Lenin instituted what he called the New Economic Policy, popularly known as NEP.

NEP was based on the principle that the Soviet Union had to develop its industry and infrastructure by any means necessary. Lenin hoped to encourage foreign capital to invest in the new nation. He also wanted to inspire as many professionals and entrepreneurs as remained within the country to contribute their skills and initiative to the Soviet economy. He increased wage differentials, gave managers and professionals increased power, and generally supported various types of individual initiative and free-market activity. His treatment of Soviet peasants also changed; instead of having grain requisitioned from them, the peasants were simply taxed.

Lenin died in 1924, leaving the two figures of Stalin and Trotsky competing for leadership of the Communist Party – and so of the nation. Trotsky had been a major revolutionary leader along with Lenin, and had commanded the Red Army during the Civil War. Stalin had only come to prominence after the Revolution, but, skilled at manipulating Party bureaucratic structures, had quickly risen in power. After Lenin's death, he gradually increased his own control over the Communist Party of the Soviet Union (CPSU) by expelling Trotsky, Grigory Zinoviev, and Lev Kamenev as left-wing opposition in 1927, and then removing Nikolai Bukharin and his associates as right-wing opposition in 1928. Then, in 1929, Stalin began his famous policy of collectivization.

COLLECTIVIZATION: THE SOVIET DILEMMA

The collectivization debates marked the first decade of Soviet history, and most historians see them as the determining factor in Soviet political economy from that time to this. The problem at first glance seemed simple: how to use the Soviet Union's main economic resource – grain – as the basis for building up its industrial base.

But a closer look shows this apparently straightforward question to be enormously complex. First, the Soviet Union was at this time virtually isolated from the rest of the Western industrialized world. The only capital available to it was what it could raise by sales of its grain. Furthermore, the Soviet Union was then the only socialist country in the world. It had already been invaded by Germany during World War I and by the Allies during the Civil War. It had every reason to believe that some nation would invade it again, particularly as it saw the rise of fascism in Italy and Nazism in Germany. This made the development of its industrial plant even more crucial, and its need for grain as the means to finance this development became essential.

Thanks to the reforms brought about by the Revolution, most Soviet farmland had been divided among peasants who were not used to producing for a market economy. If there was a surplus one year, the peasant family might eat a little better, or put grain aside for next year. They were very unlikely to market their surplus, and even less likely to mobilize themselves to unusual levels of production.

Furthermore, the Soviet system was committed to equality. If an individual peasant family did well, it might wish to expand its holdings, buying land out from neighboring peasants and turning them into employees rather than owners. This was contrary to the principles of socialism, although in the short term it might lead to increased grain surpluses becoming available.

If individual peasants were likely either to hoard their own grain or to impoverish others, what was the solution? To the early Soviet planners, the answer seemed obvious: collectivization. What could be a better solution than uniting several peasant landholdings into a single collective farm that could benefit from economies of scale while producing a profitable surplus of grain?

Many peasants did in fact welcome the prospect of collectivization. But many did not. Various Soviet economists had differing theories on how rapidly to collectivize; different segments of the CPSU had different ideas on how this plan could be implemented politically. When Stalin finally consolidated his power in 1929, he moved towards the most brutal and extreme version of collectivization – forced organization of the state farm (sovkhozes) and collective farms (kolkhozes), made possible by the infamous political terror of the secret police.

Stalin's drive for political control extended into every sector of Soviet society. As we have seen, he instituted a first wave of purges in 1927 and 1928. In 1934, he began a second wave designed to expand further his control of first the CPSU, then the society as a whole. Millions of Soviet citizens were arrested; many were killed; others were imprisoned in labor camps.

WORLD WAR II AND THE NEW POST-WAR WORLD

Some historians argue that Stalin's purges radically weakened both the armed forces and the society as a whole. Others point out that, in fact, the Soviet Union did move rapidly towards industrialization under the dictatorial leader. In either case, the years of World War II represented enormous hardship and effort of the Soviet people, many of whom worked double shifts and six-day weeks in their homefront support of "the Great Patriotic War."

During the war, Western Europe, the United States, and the Soviet Union were allies against Nazism and fascism. But after the defeat of fascism, the post-war world saw a renewed anti-Soviet effort from the United States and Europe. Even as the Soviets consolidated political control over the Eastern European countries they had liberated from the Nazis, so did the United States begin its drive to "contain" and "isolate" countries on the other side of the so-called "Iron Curtain."

These were contradictory times for the Soviet Union. On the one hand, the end of World War II meant that a much greater portion of the world had suddenly become socialist. In addition to the republics of Latvia, Lithuania, and Estonia, which were annexed to the Soviet Union, pro-Soviet socialist parties came to power in Czechoslovakia, Bulgaria, Hungary, Romania, and Albania. A socialist party took power in Yugoslavia, as well. Then, in 1949, another revolution produced a pro-Soviet socialist system – in the new People's Republic of China. Korea and Vietnam had their own Communist parties, which came to power in parts of those nations. Later, in 1959, Cuba had a revolution which soon became a Communist movement.

On the other hand, although these nations contributed to the Soviet Union's political power, they put a further strain on its economic strength. In most cases, the Soviets were contributing huge amounts of foreign aid to the new Communist countries. At the same time, they were rebuilding their destroyed industrial plants and trying to achieve military parity with the West. Still, for a time, it looked as though the Soviet economy was doing well. When Soviet premier Nikita Khrushchev made his famous remark at the United Nations – "We will bury you" – it was economic superiority he was talking about.

THE THAW AND DETENTE

Khrushchev had come to power three years after Stalin's death in 1953, after a lifetime of experience as a junior official in Stalin's bureaucracy. Years of resentment at Stalinist restrictions exploded in the famous "thaw," a time of political ferment following Khrushchev's denunciation of Stalin's crimes in his 1956 speech to the Soviet Party Congress.

For a while, political and economic reform took off under Khrushchev's leadership. Then, in 1964, the conservative wing of the CPSU moved to depose Khrushchev, replacing his with a dual leadership. The conservative Leonid Brezhnev was leader of the CPSU while the more progressive Andrei Kosygin was named Soviet premier.

Brezhnev led the Soviet Union for 18 years, both before and after the death of Kosygin. Today, ex-Soviet historians dub his period "the era of stagnation," but at the time, many believed that Brezhnev presided over accomplishments as well as setbacks. Chief among his achievements was the beginning of détente with the United States, negotiated with President Richard Nixon in 1973, as well as the gaining of nuclear parity with the United States. One of Brezhnev's major mistakes was the invasion of Afghanistan, which drained the Soviet Union of people and resources while lowering its prestige abroad and contributing to disillusionment at home.

THE END OF SOCIALISM

After the death of Brezhnev in 1982, Soviet leaders began efforts to end the era of stagnation. (For more on the economic history of this period, see the next section.) Yuri Andropov, former leader of the KGB, or Soviet secret police, took over for 15 months, initiating many new economic experiments before he died. He was followed by Konstantin Chernenko, a centrist who was careful not to rock the boat before he too died in 1985. When Mikhail Gorbachev became Party leader, the Soviet Union was ripe for political and economic reform.

For several years, it seemed as though Gorbachev's reforms would be enough to modernize the stagnating Soviet economy and to revive faith in the Soviet political system. With *perestroika* – reconstruction – his program of economic reform, and *glasnost* – openness – his program of political reform, Soviet citizens seemed to be getting excited both about improving their economy and about increasing their participation in national politics.

What Gorbachev found, however, was that opening the door to political and economic reform also meant opening the door to pro-capitalist elements in both spheres. He also found himself presiding over increased ethnic conflict among the dozens of Soviet nationalities, coupled with a growing resentment of the Russians, who many other Soviets felt had dominated national politics for too long. One by one, various Soviet republics began to press for independence from the Union while others fought for union, but on new terms.

Over the years of his presidency, Gorbachev faced tensions from all sides: would-be entrepreneurs had no commitment to socialism in any form, while old-line bureaucrats deeply opposed any kind of reform. In September 1990, Gorbachev announced a "500-Day Plan" to reform the country's economy, hoping to overcome the growing crisis. Food harvest and distribution systems had broken down, citizens were hoarding food, and black marketeers of all types were profiting from illegal trade. The legislature and the bureaucracy were too divided to support the plan; the public was too disillusioned to defend it.

Throughout the fall of 1990, food prices rose at an alarming rate. Rumors of a coup abounded and ethnic tensions increased. In 1991,

Gorbachev tried to walk a political tightrope between dissidents and hardliners. He lost a great deal of support by allowing Soviet troops to move into the Lithuanian capital, and lost further support when he extended the powers of the KGB. His moves to reform the economy – devaluing the rouble, raising prices, and invalidating 50- and 100-rouble notes to prevent hoarding – met with resistance and frustration.

In the summer of 1991, Boris Yeltsin was elected president of the Russian Republic, on a platform opposing socialism and the Soviet government. Gorbachev backed even further away from the Marxist-Leninist ideals of the socialist nation, working with Yeltsin to draft a treaty uniting the Soviet Union on a new basis.

No one can say what the future of socialism would have been had the treaty been signed. Some observers believed that, in any case, Gorbachev's support for that system had ceased and that Yeltsin's and the pro-capitalists' rise to power was already inevitable. Others believed that in his heart, Gorbachev had remained a socialist and would have found a way to return the country to some version of socialist ideals.

In any case, events took a new turn on August 19th, when, taking advantage of Gorbachev's absence from Moscow on vacation, a group of military hardliners attempted a coup. For three days, they had control of the Soviet government, promising a return to "the old days." Commentator Vladimir Pozner estimated that at least one-third of the country supported the coup – but, led by Yeltsin, the young people of Moscow took to the streets to oppose it. When the Soviet troops refused to fire upon their own people, the coup was defeated, bringing Yeltsin into a new position of power.

The end of the coup marked the end of the socialist era of the Soviet Union. The future of the Commonwealth of Independent States which former Soviet Republics have formed, remains uncertain. Clearly, Russians and other ex-Soviet republics are more eager than ever before to welcome Western investors and traders. Clearly, too, the traditions of socialism – including a persistent sense of egalitarianism, mistrust of profit-making, and a commitment to social services and workers' rights – have endured in some fashion. What the political status of the 15 former Soviet republics will be is as yet undefined, as are their economic relations with one another and with the West.

Perhaps the only certainty about the future of Russia remains its continuity with the past: the enduring legacy of tension and contradiction.

The country is still divided between admirers of the West and Slavophiles, still torn between a communal tradition and the desire for consumer goods and entrepreneurial activity, still split between its allegiances to Europe and its connections to Asia. The Westerner who wants to do business with Russia would do well to keep these contradictions in mind.

DOING BUSINESS WITH THE RUSSIANS

2

OPPORTUNITY AND CHANGE

The Western business traveler who seeks to do business in Russia finds a world of paradoxes. On the one hand, he or she will discover an enormous consumer market greedy for all types of Western goods and services, from electronic calculators to silk-screened T-shirts, from accounting techniques to fast-food restaurants. On the other hand, the foreign business person faces an economy in crisis, undergoing rampant inflation, and financed by a form of currency not readily convertible on the international market.

Likewise, the foreign business person will meet with a thorough-going enthusiasm for the "free market," for Western-style management practices and commitment to efficiency, and for infusions of foreign capital. On the other hand, he or she may encounter a seemingly intransigent opposition to firings or layoffs, to increased work quotas and speedups, and to refusals to provide the social services and "safety nets" that former Soviet citizens had come to take for granted.

To analyze effectively the prospects for economic success in Russia, the foreign business person will have to take three major factors into account: the state of the Russian economy; attitudes of the Russians toward work, business, consumption, and success; and the structures available for contacts with the West.

THE RUSSIAN ECONOMY
A Difficult Legacy

Under the old regime, the Soviet Union possessed a highly regulated economy whose detailed economic plans were regularly undermined by enormous inefficiency, corruption, and black marketeering. A fundamental principle of this planned economy was the right of Soviet citizens in general and Soviet workers in particular to employment, reasonably priced housing, basic foodstuffs, education, childcare, and medical care.

The Soviet economic system was born out of the October Revolution of 1917, during a period when the fledgling Russian industrial plant and infrastructure had been virtually destroyed by war. The primary need of this economy was to rebuild heavy industry, a need reinforced by the near-total boycott of trade with the Soviet Union by most of the industrial countries of the West. In these circumstances, Soviet leaders naturally put a high value on industrial and military self-sufficiency, a value that appeared to receive further support from the horrific destruction resulting from the German invasions of World War II. During the first few decades of Soviet history, Russian and other Soviet workers showed themselves capable of mobilization to an astonishing extent, working long hours to build and rebuild their nation's heavy-industrial capacity.

Because of their commitment to socialism, Soviet leaders put a high value on other factors as well: the guaranteed subsidy of basic social services; a wage structure that should be as egalitarian as possible; and the rights of workers to employment and to certain working conditions, even at the expense of management prerogatives.

Perhaps naturally, the lowest priority in the Soviet Union's early decades was light industry – the basis of a consumer economy. Likewise, services, a distribution system, and the other attributes of Western-style service-oriented economies were given short shrift.

In a similar vein, Russian workers were inspired to work long and hard when it seemed their country's survival was at stake – but there were virtually no other incentives to produce "above and beyond" the call of duty. In the West, workers had both the negative incentive of facing unemployment and its consequent economic hardships, and the positive incentive of the ability to accumulate consumer goods and services. Soviet/Russian workers had neither of these incentives. On the one hand, they were virtually guaranteed economic protection by their country's labor shortage as well as by its extensive "safety net" of social services. On the other hand, they were living in an economy that had virtually no interest in accommodating itselt to the consumer. They were neither fearful of poverty nor hopeful of riches. Although some might be inspired by social idealism or unusual personal ambition to work hard, offer positive suggestions for improving efficiency, or otherwise display a commitment to productivity, many were content simply to "get along" – to the detriment of their economy.

Thus when the threat of wartime and related shortages receded, the Soviet economy faced two major problems. One, its workforce was not equipped to mobilize for the high productivity that was being achieved by competitor Western economies, particularly in post-war Germany and Japan. Two, its very nature was geared to the primitive accumulation of capital and the construction of heavy industry, putting it at a distinct disadvantage in the late-twentieth century global economy. These internal problems were compounded by the post-war legacy of destruction and the continually escalating military competition with the West.

Most observers believe that the Soviet economy had a chance to modernize in the late 1960s or early 1970s. At this time, the Soviets had much-publicized triumphs in the space race and were seen to be pushing ahead in their exploration of cybernetics and computer-related studies. Yet for both political and economic reasons, the Soviets allowed the scientific-technological revolution to pass them by. Soviet leaders believed that the quest for nuclear parity and the world balance of power deserved more resources than the modernization of the Soviet economy. Furthermore, the Soviet style of restricting information made political anathema of computers, photocopiers, and other information-circulating technology.

Perestroika – Its Successes and Failures

The situation described here is most frequently associated with the long tenure of Leonid Brezhnev as General Secretary of the Soviet Communist Party, and later as Soviet Premier. After Brezhnev's death, a series of Soviet leaders attempted to address the economic stagnation that came to be seen as his legacy. Yuri Andropov, in the brief term he enjoyed before he died, began a national campaign to combat the widespread absenteeism and alcoholism that lowered the productivity of the Soviet workforce. He closed down liquor stores during working hours and began a well-publicized program of chasing workers out of *banyas* – public bathhouses – where Soviets were wont to congregate during working hours to bathe, drink beer, eat salted fish, play cards, and talk.

Mikhail Gorbachev's campaign became known as "perestroika" – literally, "restructuring." For a while, it seemed as though his programs would be successful, and he met with enormous enthusiasm, both at home and abroad. Gorbachev proposed that economic perestroika be supported by political "glasnost" – openness. He wanted to bring the fruits of the scientific-technological revolution to the Soviet Union; to attract Western capital and trade; to modify centralized planning to allow for more independence of managers; and, perhaps most importantly, to inspire the Soviet population to a new enthusiasm for efficiency, productivity, and hard work.

But Gorbachev faced a number of obstacles, difficulties whose legacy still plagues the ex-Soviet economy today. By his own count, the Soviet leader was saddled with a bureaucracy of some 18 million

Party and government officials insisting upon rigid protocol and several layers of "checks and balances" before any decision, no matter how small, could be made and implemented. Even now, with the Communist party disbanded and the government in transition, numerous problems remain: the tradition of bureaucratic delays and inefficiencies; the unwieldy structures that have yet to be replaced; and the mere physical existence of millions of bureaucrats for whom employment will have to be found as the structures that supported them are refashioned.

Then, too, Gorbachev struggled with the restrictions of the Soviet labor market. Government estimates showed that some three million Soviets were thrown out of work between 1985 and 1989, as Gorbachev worked to modernize and streamline his country's economy. Before Gorbachev's fall, he had estimated that some 15 million more jobs would be eliminated by the century's end. In the new free-for-all "open" economy, it is likely that even more jobs will disappear. Not only will foreign business people have to contend with the specter of widespread unemployment – a condition hardly likely to lend itself to increased consumption of Western goods. In addition, foreign investors will have to deal with a labor market in flux, an unstable economy in which workers have not necessarily received the training most in demand.

Another traditional Soviet problem was the lack of a decent system of distribution, which meant that even when the economy was producing goods, consumers often had no access to them. A *Newsday* article by Alison Mitchell, published at the very end of 1990, reported on a situation that typifies the problem.

Mitchell wrote her article at the time of the first rationing in the city of Leningrad (now St. Petersburg) since World War II. She described Leningrad city councillors charged with investigating food shortages as they entered a warehouse – and found huge stacks of boxes, including Chinese canned meat and powdered milk, some of which had been sitting there for months. In addition, they found 28 shipping container loads of coffee, languishing in port, despite shortages of this popular beverage throughout the city. Some 902,000 tons of lamb and pork had arrived from Germany in the first week of December – and five days later, a great deal of it was still undistributed. Although a nearby truck depot had detailed two trucks a day to haul meat, some five or six trucks a day were assigned to haul furniture. The councillors were unable to determine who was responsible for that decision, an inexplicable inefficiency only too common in the old Soviet Union – and, perhaps, still common today.

Further, the Soviets had a decades-long tradition of guaranteed employment, social services, and subsidies. Despite the housing shortage, rents were low. A one-room apartment could cost as little as 15 roubles a month – less than 10% of a monthly salary. A good-sized place could run as high as 30 roubles a month – but that still added up to little more than three days' pay per month for most workers. Health care and education were free; basic foodstuffs such as bread, milk, potatoes, and cheese were subsidized; and most Soviet workers preferred rationing and long queues to the price increases and inequalities of an "open market." As Gorbachev opened the door to the West, he allowed Soviet citizens to become ever more aware of Western-style consumer goods and lifestyles. But the same Soviet citizens who coveted this lifestyle and resented their own system for not providing it were not necessarily willing to give up the privileges that they enjoyed in its place.

In the same vein, Soviet citizens prized their protected employment. In an October 28, 1990, *New York Times Magazine* article, Soviet expert Hedrick Smith quotes Rair Simonyan, Gorbachev's head of industrial management at Moscow's Institute of International Relations and World Economy. Simonyan described his own efficiency experts' reluctance to recommend sweeping changes in the Soviet economy, claiming that they made such statements as "You cannot fire a man in his fifties with no job prospects or a woman with two children." These attitudes ran counter to Gorbachev's later efforts to "westernize" the Soviet economy, and certainly are factors that a contemporary business investor would have to take into account.

The tradition of collectivity and social responsibility, and the related distrust of profit, go back to the founder of the Soviet Union, Lenin himself. In 1918, Lenin wrote, "We consider the land to be common property. But if I take a piece...for myself, cultivate twice as much grain as I need and sell the excess at a profit...am I really behaving like a Communist? No. I am behaving like an exploiter, like a proprietor." Soviets steeped in such thinking were hardly likely to respond well to Gorbachev's introduction of Western economic ideas – nor will they be receptive to Western-style management and investment today.

Finally, Gorbachev had to contend with the widespread corruption that riddled the Soviet system, from the huge underground black market that dealt in Western consumer goods and currency; to the petty and not-so-petty pilfering common in virtually every sector of Soviet society; to the bureaucratic kickbacks and theft at all levels of government and industry.

Soviet corruption did not only take the form of stealing. Lying was also a problem. In Uzbekistan, for example, the Soviet textile republic, Gorbachev's investigators found that every year the republic had reported one million tons of cotton harvest to the central government – a million tons that simply did not exist. Such deception naturally made a mockery of any attempt at economic planning. Once again, this legacy haunts Russia and the ex-Soviet republics today, as officials struggle to assemble accurate information about industrial plant capacity, output, and costs.

Current Assessments

As we saw in the previous section, it is the period after the August coup that has provided the greatest opportunities for Western businesses. And it is during this period that we find both the most optimistic and the most pessimistic accounts of such prospects. In general, Western businesses who have already begun investing in or trading with the Soviet Union present a positive business outlook – even while cautioning their colleagues about certain difficulties.

Jeffrey Hertzfeld, a Paris-based American lawyer who works with Western investors in the Soviet Union, sums up the paradox in a September 1, 1991, *New York Times* article written by Steven Greenhouse: "If you wait until you have an ideal investment environment, with clear laws and rules of the game, you're talking five or ten years," Hertzfeld says. "But if you wait five years, you might find that a lot of the most attractive partners have already made commitments to other companies."

Ronald Freeman, quoted in the same article, agrees that Western investors would do well to take advantage of the openings offered by the coup's failure. Freeman is the First Vice President of the European Bank for Reconstruction and Development, a new London-based bank set up to rebuild business in Eastern Europe. "The coup's failure has galvanized a rapidly growing desire to get on with the conversion to a market economy," Freeman says. "Everyone, at every level of government, seems to be pointing in that direction."

The experience of the Dallas-based Dresser Industries, a manufacturer of oilfield equipment, is probably instructive as to both the pros and the cons of doing business with the ex-Soviet Union. Dresser Chairman John J. Murphy was optimistic as quoted in the September 1991 *New York Times* article: "Within the Russian republic, I think things will accelerate very quickly, and that should also be true for the Ukraine. The people who were blocking reform are gone."

Yet Dresser faced a number of problems in its efforts to receive the contract to rebuild a drill-bit factory located in southern Russia. In the old Soviet Union, a number of government entities claimed jurisdiction and the right to award the contract. Various ministries at both the national and the republic level were involved in the decision – and many of the relevant ministries lacked the hard currency needed to complete the deal!

Alcatel, a Paris-based telecommunications company, faced similar obstacles. Alcatel wanted to invest in a factory in St. Petersburg (then Leningrad) to make digital switching equipment. The French company was prepared to invest $3.5 billion in equipment over a twenty-year period. Yet the project nearly foundered in a bureaucratic sea of conflicting jurisdictions. The City of Leningrad owned the land on which the factory was built, while the Soviet Ministry of Industry was responsible for the plant's actual construction – and the plant itself was operated by the Soviet Army! In addition, the Soviet ministries of telecommunication and machinery were involved in finalizing plans, as were the Russian Republic's Ministries of Telecommunications and Machinery, as well as several Leningrad city departments. Even now that the national structure has been dismantled and the republic structure is in flux, Western investors may find that the "spirit is willing," but the bureaucratic apparatus is weak.

Additionally, the rouble – the basic unit of currency in the Soviet Union – is considered virtually worthless abroad. Foreign investors will probably prefer the recent decision by Russia and other republics to float the rouble on the international market, rather than retain its protected but unconvertible status. Nevertheless, the unfavorable exchange rate may deter some foreign businesses.

Foreign investors cite other economic problems. Despite the opportunities offered by the failure of the coup, the ex-Soviet Union's industrial output was expected to drop 30% in 1991. The country already suffered from rampant inflation, which is expected to worsen as the rouble falls in value. Soviet daily oil output has dropped some 20% since 1988, largely due to aging equipment and poor management – with no immediate prospects for improvement in sight.

Foreign experts on Russian/Soviet business cite further difficulties. The telecommunications system in the ex-Soviet Union is extremely poor by Western standards. Apartments and office space in the major cities of Moscow and Leningrad are both expensive and difficult to obtain. And the promised market reforms planned by Russian President Boris Yeltsin as well as by the leaders of other republics are not yet completely in place. According to a September 1991 *New York Times* article, "… many American and Japanese officials still maintain that until market reforms are in place, giving massive aid would be like pouring money down a sinkhole."

Yet there is a brighter side. Investors dealing in particular industries have been able to take advantage of the ex-Soviet Union's wealth of oil, gas, and minerals. Despite the oil industry's decline, for example, the ex-Soviet Union's output is still the largest in the world. To quote Murphy once again, "If you simply look at what needs to be done to increase production from known oil reservoirs, that is probably the greatest single opportunity in the world for our industry. If you look at new exploration opportunities, where there are known geological structures that are promising or at drilling, you double or triple that opportunity." Thus Chevron, Texaco, and British Petroleum, among others, would like to develop joint ventures with ex-Soviet oil enterprises.

Companies interested in investing in gas or other natural resources can also benefit from Russian bounty. These resources are most easily converted into hard currency through foreign sales, offering foreigners further protection on their investment. Kazakhstan and the Ukraine also possess vast natural resources of interest to foreign investors.

Businesses dealing in consumer goods may also find green pastures in the ex-Soviet Union. Such industries will probably do best in the populous regions of Russia (150 million inhabitants) and the Ukraine (another 52 million people) – roughly the equivalent of the population of France. Together, these two republics include some 70% of the population of the ex-Soviet Union.

Consumer services are another fertile field of opportunity. The Radisson Hotel recently entered into a 430-room joint-venture establishment in Moscow. "The people we have been dealing with in the Russian Federation – at the city council level and the republic level – are already in the progressive mode and want to do business in a different way," said John A. Nordlander, corporation president, quoted in the September 1991 *New York Times* article. Likewise, the Marriott chain, McDonald's, and Pizza Hut have begun Russian deals that look to be extremely lucrative.

Generally, foreign observers advise the Western business investor/trader to think in terms of decades, rather than years. "What is at stake here is not a simple reform," warns Alexander Vacic, chief economist for the United Nations' Economic Commission for Europe in Geneva. "It is the alteration of an entire economic system to a completely different system, for which the population does not have the preparation and towards which it has animosity in many cases."

George Hamilton, Senior Managing Director of International Business Development for Polaroid, agrees that Western investors must take the long view. "Companies that worry only about taking out short-term profits can feed the nation's distrust of capitalism that started one hundred years ago," he says. "We see the Soviet Union as a long-term commitment."

RUSSIAN ATTITUDES

Most foreign business travelers to Russia are struck by the cultural differences between Russia and the West. Some of these differences are rooted in Russia's centuries-long history of isolation, poverty, and arrested economic development. Others are the more recent product of Russia's decades-long experience of socialism. Although generalizations and cultural stereotypes are always problematic, experienced Western observers do note some patterns that they have come to expect in their business dealings with Russia.

The "Russian Soul"

For the past three centuries, Russian writers have tried to define what they are fond of calling "the Russian soul" – that unique blend of melancholy, passion, and spirituality described by such writers as Tolstoy, Gogol, and Dostoevsky. Here are two quotes from modern writers, cited by Hedrick Smith in his *New York Times Magazine* article of October 28, 1990:

"Russian mentality is not based on common sense. It has nothing to do with common sense. Our thinking is not orderly, logical. In Western culture, European culture maybe, emotion is considered to be on a lower level than reason. But in Russia, no. It is bad to be rational, to be smart, clever, intelligent, and so on. And to be emotional, warm, lovable, maybe spiritual, in the full meaning of that word – that is good."

– Tatyana Tolstaya

"It is the Russian soul. In Russia, I think we have a love of literature, a so-called spiritual life. We can talk all day and all night long about all kinds of questions, immortal questions. That is the Russian style of thinking. I want our economy to be the same as in the West. I want our people to have a good quality of life, a good level, the same as in America, and technology as in Japan and America. But I am afraid to lose this Russian part of our soul, to lose our love of literature and…how to put it…our impractical character. Maybe too lazy, it is a minus, but a plus, too."

– Andrei Voznesensky

Both Voznesensky and Tolstaya suggest that for Russians, relationships matter more than anything else – certainly far more than efficiency, the accumulation of material possessions, or the achievement of individual success. This value is expressed by three closely related Russian words that can be used to describe a person's character – with increasing degrees of disapproval. To call a person *sukhovaty* – "dryish" – is bad enough. That's the type of word that might be used to describe a person who lacks the "Russian soul," a person who is somewhat immune to the grand passions that sway more sympathetic types. However, it's still worse to call a person *sukhoi* – "dry." That's the type of word one might use to describe a lawyer or perhaps a bureaucrat, someone whose vital juices have gradually been drained away. But to call a person *sukhar* – that's the worst of all. Someone who is *sukhar* is dry as a bone, or as an old stale crust of bread – a person who has no human feeling left at all. While many Westerners might have ambivalent feelings toward the *sukhar* individual whose single-minded ambition has made him or her a financial success, most Russians would have no ambivalence at all. They would regard such a person with a shudder of disgust and a wish to avoid any possibility of sharing that quality.

The Communal Tradition

To some extent, this valuing of feelings and relationships comes from the collective and communal traditions that Russians have known for hundreds of years, first under tsarism and later under socialism. Most Russian peasants never lived on individual homesteads. Instead, they lived in an *obshchina* – literally, a "society" – in which houses were huddled close together and land spread out around.

This communal form had enormous vitality, surviving throughout the ages in various forms. Serfdom – the medieval form of near-slavery linking a group of peasants to a particular plot of land and to a particular overlord – was not abolished in Russia until 1861. And even after peasants were technically free to leave their land, most continued to live in the form of a commune, or *mir*. Significantly, the Russian word can mean "commune," "world," "peace," *and* "universe." In Russian society, the *mir* was the peasant's world, a communal form in which peasants decided collectively how to assign land, when to plant, when to harvest, and how to work the fields. Typically, each family would get some good land and some not so good, so that the residents of the *mir* would share a common fate, standing or falling together with each good harvest, or each bad winter.

After the Revolution of 1917, peasants continued to constitute the vast majority of the Russian population for many decades. And they continued to live communally, on state or collective farms. In this context, a person's relationships with his or her neighbors were not just an aspect of "the good life" – they were life itself. Certainly, these relationships were far more important than individual ambition or accumulation of riches.

The positive side of this communal life was the generosity, hospitality, warmth, and passionate friendship that it nurtured. The negative side was the enormous resentment that many Russians experienced against anyone who stood out from the crowd in any way, particularly against anyone who achieved any degree of individual material success. "Remember, the tallest blade of grass is the first to be cut down by the scythe," goes one peasant saying.

Another old joke goes even further in depicting the envy and suspicion that a Russian might feel for a prosperous neighbor. As the story goes, God offers a Russian peasant any reward the peasant desires – on the condition that the peasant's neighbor will receive double the reward. The peasant racks his brains, trying to think of how he can benefit himself without doubly benefiting his neighbor. Finally, he has the solution: he tells God to take away one of his eyes, knowing that this will make his neighbor totally blind.

Americans or British people who visit Russia have noticed a more colloquial version of this trait. When they are asked the routine question, "How are you," they will nearly always answer "Fine," or even "Great!" even if, in fact, they've just had a run of bad luck. In Russia, though, it is just the opposite. Most Russians, when asked how they are, will most likely say, "OK," or "Not too bad," even if they've just been given a promotion or moved into the apartment of their dreams. After all, why tempt fate – or provoke others – by bragging about your good fortune?

This communal tradition goes far toward explaining a paradox that many foreigners have noticed on trips to Russia and elsewhere in the ex-Soviet Union. Many Russians can be extremely hospitable and generous. If they have decided that you are a friend, or a guest, they are capable of sharing their last precious store of fresh fruit, or of using up the last of that month's spending money to buy you a ticket to the opera. At the same time, foreigners might notice a mean-spirited and competitive streak in Russians as they engage in bitter fights with fellow customers over the last of the rationed meat or scarce coffee. For people who are considered to be "inside the circle" – even foreigners or strangers who have been recently met and welcomed – the typical Russian will do anything, will share his or her belongings down to the last crust of bread or spend a month's salary on a birthday party or a parting gift. For people who are "outside the circle" – which might include every other shopper in the market and the salesclerk as well – hostility, envy, and a no-holds-barred attitude are the rule.

Work and Success

Of course, there are plenty of Russians who don't fit the pattern described here. Particularly since the failure of the coup in August 1991, Russia has seen an increasing number of ambitious entrepreneurs – some of whom are former black marketeers now turned independent owners, result-oriented engineers and enterprise managers who worked equally hard under the old system, and the new get-ahead bureaucrats and Party officials who amassed huge illegal fortunes under the old system by dint of unremitting, albeit illicit, efforts.

But in a very real sense, these figures are the exceptions that prove the rule. Their very ambition and individualism stand in striking contrast to the qualities of the vast majority of Russians. And, for this very reason, they are the targets of enormous hostility and contempt, under the new system as well as the old.

Though the Russians have expressed their overwhelming desire for an economic system that offers the consumerist rewards of the West, they have just as vehemently expressed their unwillingness to pay some of the prices that go with those rewards. For example, even in the final days of perestroika, there were attacks on farmers, privately owned cooperative restaurants, and small service shops. The successes, however small, of these tiny businesses meant something very different in Russia from what they would have in the West. To an American, for example, a small business success represents a validation of the "American dream," proof that anyone who works hard can "make it" (even if in reality, the vast majority of small businesses fail within five years). To a Russian, a business success, even a small one, means that someone else is being exploited.

Although Russians welcomed the goods and services provided by perestroika's new entrepreneurs, they also accused them of taking advantage of others. At the Supreme Soviet, throughout Gorbachev's presidency, deputies continually charged that introducing the "free market" would allow speculators to get rich at workers' expense. Although Soviet workers wanted more consumer goods, they had a horror of floating prices and deeply opposed an end to subsidies – let alone a reduction in social services or an end to guaranteed employment.

Along with Russians' ambivalence toward consumerism and success comes an ambivalence toward what in the West is known as the "work ethic." This is the philosophy that hard work is a kind of virtue in itself, leading inevitably both to material success and to a kind of moral superiority.

In Russia, on the other hand, work is not prized for its own sake, and the goal of material success is in any case regarded as a questionable one. A common Russian joke under perestroika was, "They pretend to pay us, and we pretend to work."

Of course, as we have seen, Russians and other ex-Soviets were capable of tremendous hard work during World War II and during periods of reconstruction after both world wars. In fact, the voluntary double shifts and six-day weeks of Soviet workers during those periods are almost unimaginable to many inhabitants of the West. Yet these were *collective* work projects, engaged in with one's neighbors and fellow citizens, either to protect one's homeland from a clear threat or to rebuild a nation out of wartime devastation. Something of the same spirit obtained in the collective projects once sponsored by Komsomol, the Communist youth group, in which groups of students would go together to Siberia or other underdeveloped regions and literally build an entire community out of nothing. The enthusiasm and joy of the "pioneering spirit" certainly existed in the Soviet Union – but generally not in the form of individual enterprise.

The collective approach to work was certainly fostered by many elements in the old Soviet system. For example, young Russians frequently lived at home for many years while they attended university. Whereas many Westerners would go away to college, living on their own in dormitories or even their own apartments, living at home under parental guidance and support was far more common in the Soviet Union. For this reason, most Soviets did not begin earning money until after graduation.

The different nature of work continued past the college years. In the West, every college student studies under the specter of the need to find a job, if not now, then after graduation. In the old Soviet Union, however, students enjoyed the system of *raspredeleniye* – "distribution." For the first three years after graduation, they were assigned to a job in their chosen field, wherever they were most needed. This system worked both ways: students could relax in the knowledge that they would have a chance to do the work they had trained for, and they could feel secure in the knowledge that they were serving the collective good rather than working for their private ambition. What might be lost in individual effort and initiative was supposed to have been made up in service to the collective.

Today, many Russians experience a mixture of attitudes toward work, business, consumption, and success. On the one hand, they have grown up with the collective traditions of their history and their former system, traditions that have fostered both positive and negative qualities. On the other hand, they have experienced enormous disillusionment with many aspects of their former system and its traditions without really having come into much contact with opposing systems from the West. How Russians will negotiate their new circumstances remain to be seen. Most Russian entrepreneurs, at least, would agree that the renowned writer Maxim Gorky's remarks remain all too apropos. When revolutionary leader Lenin asked Gorky why he chose to remain in exile, Gorky is supposed to have replied, "You know, Vladimir Ilyich, at home in Russia they all go around and shake each other's hands and talk all the time and swap anecdotes. No one really works."

Some seventy years later, then Deputy Mayor of Moscow, Stankevich, made a statement only slightly more optimistic. As quoted by Francis X. Clines in a March 8, 1991, *New York Times Magazine* piece, Stankevich said, "So far there is no clear understanding of what democracy is. Many people think it gives birth to goods and services, and all they have to do is consume them. It's a classic attitude. 'We voted for you. Now give us everything.' Only a small part of the voters say, 'We want you to create conditions for us to act freely, and we will do the rest.' "

MAKING DEALS IN THE NEW RUSSIA
Great Opportunities

Within the borders of the former Soviet Union are some 285 million consumers. At this point in their economic development, they face shortages of nearly every consumer luxury that has come to be taken for granted in the West: televisions, VCRs, watches, radios, CD players, refrigerators, microwaves, and the like.

On the other hand, the fifteen former Soviet republics make up the largest land mass in the world, possessing enormous riches in the form of natural resources: gold, silver, diamonds, platinum, chromium, petroleum, and natural gas. Russia alone possesses stretches of timber that add up to the size of North America. The former Soviet Union was an exporter of metals, minerals, petroleum, petrochemicals, heavy machinery, capital goods, forest and marine products, and advanced technology.

In the past, the Soviet Union was an importer of advanced equipment, machinery, and agricultural products. In the future, the former republics promise to be importers of consumer goods as well. Furthermore, over the past five years, before and after the fall of socialism, Russians have been increasingly interested in importing Western technology, management techniques, business services – and, primarily, capital.

In this context, the Western business person can do extremely well, if he or she is careful, knowledgeable, and persistent. The first step is to identify the types of business that will be profitable in the short- and the long-term.

Joint Ventures

The most widely publicized deals with Russia and other ex-Soviet republics in recent months have been joint ventures: projects that are financed jointly by Russian and Western businesses and companies of the ex-Soviet republics. These ventures first began to be seen after the new Gorbachev-sponsored legislation of January 13, 1987, which broke a seventy-year precedent against foreign investment within Soviet borders by creating the legal possibility of a single enterprise being jointly owned by Soviet and foreign entities.

Although conditions have changed radically since this new legislation was first enacted, the reasons that inspired it remain in force: a need for foreign capital, equipment, know-how, management, and marketing techniques, as well as the need for foreign exchange to off-set the soft currency of the rouble.

As with all structures discussed in this volume, no one knows for certain what the final form of the joint ventureship will be. The legal and political conditions in Russia and its former republics are changing almost daily, and will certainly have undergone major transformations even while this volume is in press. Under the original legislation, the joint ownership was limited to a particular term of time, after which the enterprise reverted to total Soviet control. Conditions under the new system have yet to be fully worked out. However, it seems likely that, as things are going, conditions for foreign investors and traders in Russia can only improve, at least as far as legal and business arrangements are concerned. (Whether the Russian economy will continue to make such deals profitable is anybody's guess.)

In the past, joint ventures were entered into by the Soviets when they believed that they would enable the eventual export of Soviet goods and services, bringing hard currency into the economy. Foreign businesses, on the other hand, tended to be most interested in joint ventures that they believed would give them access to the Soviet consumer market. Clearly, the interests of the two parties tended to be diametrically opposed, although there was apparently plenty of room for compromise and profitable negotiations on both sides. Currently, the situation is changing so rapidly that it is impossible to predict on what basis joint venture deals will be available. Certainly, however, current governments are likely to be more receptive than the former socialist system, both because of increased economic desperation and because of a greater tolerance for profit-making in general.

Imports and Exports

In the past, hard currency was only available for priority imports. Thus, foreign companies who wanted to reach the great untapped Soviet consumer market had to invent imaginative trades and barters to work around government reluctance to allot money for consumer goods. PepsiCo., Inc., for example, received payment for the goods produced by its Soviet bottling plants and Pizza Hut restaurants in the form of Stolichnaya vodka and Soviet-made ships.

Currently, import regulations have loosened considerably, but hard currency availability is still a problem. Although Russian consumers are eager to buy many Western-produced goods, and although in many cases they still have considerable savings left over from the time of goods shortages, their money may not mean much to a Western business. Furthermore, rampant inflation and the lifting of price subsidies, coupled with the end of guaranteed employment, may erode Russian consumers' buying power to an unprecedented extent.

One major demand of the Russians is for advanced technology, as ex-Soviet enterprises struggle to bring their plants into the late twentieth century. However, although Western attitudes toward Russia have softened considerably, Western exporters must be careful not to run foul of domestic regulations designed to keep technological resources from falling into the hands of "enemies."

As business and political relations between the West and the Soviet Union improved, before and after the fall of socialism, many foreign companies saw the possibility for increased import business with Russia and its post-coup republics. However, U.S. tariffs on Russian imports remain extremely high, a holdover from the days of the Cold War. The Jackson-Vanik Amendment of 1974 denied most-favored-nation status to the Soviet Union in protest against Soviet laws against emigration, making much Soviet import business simply unprofitable. Although this amendment can and has been waived within bilateral trade agreements, the import situation has remained largely unfavorable. This, coupled with the generally low quality of Russian exports, has made the import side of Russian trade generally less attractive. However, when China began increasing its exports to the West in the 1970s, the quality of its goods improved rapidly, and possibly this will be the case with Russian products as well.

Market Research

Clearly, any company seeking to do either trade or investment business with the ex-Soviet Union will need to do considerable market research before deciding how to proceed. Various federal agencies may be helpful in this regard, particularly the U.S. Department of Commerce. For agricultural products, the U.S. Department of Agriculture can be helpful. In addition, industry trade associations, conferences, university-sponsored seminars, Russian trade fairs, Western trade fairs to which Russians send observers, and the various publications discussed elsewhere in this volume can be valuable sources of information.

Agencies and Consulting Firms

There are also an increasing number of independent consulting firms and agencies that are set up explicitly to help Western companies do business with Russian enterprises. While working with a consultant or agent can be extremely helpful, foreign business people should proceed with caution. The following guidelines may prove helpful:

1. Ask for references. Particularly in this period, companies claiming expertise in Russian business seem to be springing up overnight. It's important to know that the consultant or agent chosen is credible and reliable.

2. Get an estimate of charges ahead of time, and be sure there is a written agreement that lays out duties and obligations of both parties, putting a ceiling on expenses in some form. The cost of doing business with the Russians is hard to estimate in advance. Negotiations may drag on for an unspecified length of time; regulations may change while discussions are in progress; the lack of a good telecommunications or fax system makes communication with the home country more than usually difficult. For all of these reasons, an agent may rightly point out that his or her efforts to open doors for a Western firm cannot be evaluated in advance. But precisely because the situation is so uncertain, the client company must be more than usually vigilant about overseeing the agent's activity and expenses.

3. Make sure the consultant or agent is not dealing with your competitors. In such a wide-open market, it's hard to keep track of what other firms are doing. If possible, a firm employing a consultant or agent should get a written list of the other clients, to guard against conflict of interest in advance. If this is not possible, the firm should at least require written assurance that no competitors are fellow clients.

4. Arrange to pay the consultant or agent "on commission," as some kind of percentage of sales or investment. Some consultants or agents will insist on monthly retainers, but it is obviously to a firm's advantage to tie the agency's fees to its successes, particularly in a climate so rife with uncertainty.

5. Be careful about promising "exclusivity" to any consultant or agent. Some firms acting as agents for Western business want the exclusive right to make deals for those companies, particularly if their payment is being received on a commission basis. However, business contacts are made in a variety of ways, through a variety of sources. If a foreign company is able to benefit from its own efforts as well as from those of an agent or consultant, it should not be penalized.

6. Make the ability to cancel "without cause" part of the written agreement with the agent and consultant; specify the cut-off point for when commissions are owed. Because conditions in Russia are so uncertain, an agent or consultant could reasonably claim to be working hard for many months, with negotiations stalled for reasons beyond its control. If a company is dissatisfied with its agent or consultant, however, there may come a time when reasonable explanations come to sound like excuses. Although a foreign company may not be able to document that it is terminating a contract "for cause," it should be free to do so. Some formula should be agreed upon ahead of time to account for sales or profits that come in after termination – which the agents might reasonably claim to have been a result of their activity and therefore subject to their commissions.

The Business Proposal

Once a company has identified which Russian enterprises will be the most profitable trading or investment partners, the next step is to make a business proposal. Although occasionally the Russian firm will initiate contact, usually the initiative must come from the West. The following suggestions may be helpful in preparing a proposal for a Russian audience:

1. Create an entirely new proposal with a Russian audience in mind. The initial expense will prove well worth it if the deal goes through. Western firms should remember that, even under the new system, conditions are quite different in the ex-socialist world from those in the West. Sending a standard prospectus or boilerplate proposal is likely to miss several key concerns of a Russian partner, such as how currency transactions will be handled, what labor standards will be in force, and to what extent technology will be shared with the host country.

2. Prepare copies of everything in both Russian and English. The delay involved in allowing for the Russian recipient to find a translator will probably prove more costly than the expense of a translator. Furthermore, a Western firm has no assurance of how competent the Russian translator may be when it comes to technical or financial intricacies. Better to have control over the translation process than to risk misunderstandings later.

3. Don't worry about an elaborate presentation. Russian standards for business proposals are quite different from those in the West. A soft-cover binding over a neatly typed proposal is all that is required.

4. Bind or attach all materials into a single document. The fewer pieces a proposal has, the less chance that any will be mislaid. This consideration is even more important when dealing with Russia than elsewhere: 1) the telecommunications and faxes that might otherwise be used to clear up misunderstandings and to supplement missing materials are not very efficient in today's Russia; 2) even under the new system, there are still several layers of bureaucracy through which a proposal must pass. Keeping all pieces of a document under a single cover minimizes the chances of loss.

5. Make many copies of your proposal and circulate it as widely as possible. Although no one really knows the "chain of command" under the new system, Western firms would do well to research all possible parties to a deal and to supply each with a copy of the proposal. Copying facilities in Russia are primitive by Western standards, and the mails are slow and uncertain, even within a single enterprise or government office. The Western firm that circumvents this problem is one step ahead of the game.

6. Describe your proposal as clearly and concretely as possible, but make it clear that you are also open to alternative proposals from them. Russians are used to doing things in their own way.

Furthermore, the post-socialist system is still so new and the economy in such disarray that Russians are still "making things up as they go along." Ideally, a proposal should make it as easy as possible for the Russian side to express further interest, either because they like the details of the original proposal or because they see a clear shot at a counter-offer.

7. Invite inquiries and responses with clear instructions on how to be reached by telex, fax, or telephone. Although telecommunications facilities in Russia are not up to Western standards, they do exist. Clear instructions on how to respond will improve the chances of a speedy answer.

8. Suggest a follow-up meeting in Russia as soon as appropriate. Traditionally, business negotiations with the Russians are long-drawn-out affairs. Although this may change somewhat under the new system, it's usually up to the Western partner to press for speed.

Negotiations

The actual negotiations process, whether for an investment deal or a trade agreement, will almost certainly take place in Russia. Russians have no hard currency to pay their own expenses at a Western hotel, so they expect foreigners to come to them. At some point in the nego-tiating process, however, Russians may wish to come to the West, per-haps to visit their partner's business facility. In such a case, although the Russians may buy their own tickets on Aeroflot, Westerners will be expected to cover the rest of their expenses.

Traditionally, negotiations with American or English-speaking Canadian firms are conducted in English. Interpreters are usually pro-vided by the Russians, but a Western firm may want to find or bring interpreters of its own, to be sure that technical and financial terms are being properly translated. Most Russians, particularly those at high levels of government and business, speak a good deal of English. Although this makes socializing more pleasant, it will probably not be relied upon for business dealings.

Most Westerners who have had business dealings with the Russians find them to be good negotiators. Despite the contradictory Cold War myths of the Russians as either primitive children or wily evil geniuses, the truth of the matter is that they're simply people, who, like any other parties to a negotiation, want to give as little as possible while getting as much as possible. A Western firm that sends its team into negotiations with the usual amount of preparation and information will find little difference between talks with Russians and any other business meeting.

According to the old laws, any legally constituted entity from the West could be a party to business dealings; this situation will probably continue. Furthermore, the Russians have no problem with a decision in midstream to change the negotiating party from the corporation itself to one of its subsidiaries or affiliates. Any entity that is legally and economically able to provide the goods, services, or capital that the Russians seek will be welcomed as a business partner.

Soviet law, in its turn, had also allowed any legal entity to negotiate with the West, including all-union and state government agencies, cooperatives, institutes, and individual enterprises. In all likelihood, this situation will also continue, as "free enterprise" spreads throughout the former socialist nation.

Protocols and Letters of Intent

Before negotiations begin and as they proceed, Western firms may find it useful to draft letters of intent, or protocols expressing the sense of both sides' positions as they understand it. The Russians may also draft their own letters of intent.

Typically, these are short, relatively informal documents of no more than five double-spaced typewritten pages. They are not legally binding, although they are usually signed by both sides to express recognition of the accuracy of the content. These documents usually include the following points:

- mutual objectives
- main decisions that have been reached
- date, place, and agenda for the next meeting
- which side will prepare the initial contract
- how responsibility for the feasibilty study will be allocated, in terms of both doing the work and covering the expenses.

In the past, upper levels of government and Party agencies usually received copies of each protocol.

Feasibility Studies

Traditionally, the Soviets required a feasibility study before any deal could be approved. This document demonstrated the commercial, technical, and financial viability of any business arrangement with the

West. Although laws are changing rapidly, such a study may still be needed by the government or private entities doing business abroad.

Typically, a feasibility study comes out of the technical and commercial talks used to arrive at a final agreement. It generally includes the following elements:

- a clear identification of all parties to the agreement and a definition of their responsibilities in the deal
- a summary of the purpose and scope of the agreement
- financial and technical projections; e.g., planned production, marketing, or sales
- a statement of the financial arrangements: each party's financial responsibility; in what form payments must be made; how roubles will be converted; how profits will be calculated and divided; how prices will be established and converted between currencies; which tax laws of either country will apply; what accounting methods will be used; what start-up costs will be and how they will be divided; what arrangements will be made for loans and interest payments; whether and how a plant will eventually be repatriated into a wholly-owned Russian entity
- an identification of the materials needed and a statement of how they will be obtained
- in the case of a joint venture, a description of the facility, labor force, management system, and any other relevant information about daily operations
- a schedule
- reasons why the Russians should approve this deal.

The Final Agreement

Generally, the Russian partner will not object to the Western entity drafting the final agreement, contract, or charter that will be used. Although such an arrangement may be costly, it may also give the Western partner more control over the final document. Traditionally, Soviets have insisted upon sticking to the letter of any agreement, so it behooves a firm to do research into the nature of other documents with Russian partners; a firm's standard agreement may have to be adapted to specify particular points of special interest to the Russians.

Advertising

Before the breakup of the Soviet Union, there was no commercial advertising permitted. Western visitors remarked on the billboards filled with political slogans and images, rather than with consumerist appeals.

Now that situation is changing rapidly, although it is still unclear how the Russians will react to advertising as we know it in the West. At present ex-Soviet newspapers, radios, and television stations are not set up to accept advertising, nor are there commercially available billboards or public spaces designed for ads.

Enterprising companies may be finding solutions to this problem, however. Even under the old system, PepsiCo had bought some television time and planned a filming schedule in the Soviet Union. And the famous advertising agency, B.B.D. & O., recently opened a joint-venture office in Moscow. In advertising, as in so many other areas, the Russian embrace of the West may be only a matter of time.

NEWS SOURCES

Although there is an increasing number of independent publications within the ex-Soviet Union itself, Western newsletters and reports still probably provide the most useful information to foreign investors and traders desiring to do business in Russia and the other republics. Following are some of the most highly recommended publications for the business traveler:

- *Business Eastern Europe* is published by Business International, based in Vienna. This weekly newsletter is considered practical and informative by informed observers, who appreciate its reports on business ventures throughout Eastern Europe. It includes both concrete information, such as listings of trade fairs and reports on trade news of specific industries. It also offers case studies of various aspects of international business, such as joint ventures, licensing, and countertrade, as well as advice and pointers of all types.

- *East European Market,* published by the London *Financial Times,* comes out every two weeks, also reporting on Eastern Europe as a whole. Major trade deals are covered in this newsletter, as well as case studies and general financial news.

- *Soviet Business and Trade Newsletter* comes out of Washington, D.C., published by Welt Publishing. This biweekly publication focuses on practical information such as listings of contacts and exhibitions. It also reports on trade opportunities, analyzes economic developments and trends, and carries interviews with trade officials.

- *Interflo* is published in Maplewood, New Jersey, as a monthly digest of U.S. and other countries' press reports on trade with the East.

- *PlanEcon Report* is published in Washington, D.C., and is one of the best available sources for analysis of macroeconomic trends in Soviet trade, debt, and industrial development. It is an excellent source of statistics that comes out several times a year.

Foreign business travelers might also want to consult the publications of their country's Chamber of Commerce. They may also wish to ask Russian embassy officials or the Russian Studies department at their local university to recommend specialized Russian journals that cover their industry.

ARRIVING AT THE AIRPORT

3

CUSTOMS

The main concern of the business traveler arriving in Russia will be customs. Although customs regulations and practices are changing as the overall political situation changes, accurate records are still important to the business traveler and are probably his or her best safeguard against any inconvenience when leaving the country.

Upon arrival in Russia, all visitors are asked to fill out a customs declaration form to record currency and valuables and to determine the difference between personal possessions – which are duty-free – and imports for sale – which are, of course, taxed. The business traveler will need this customs declaration upon departure, so that Russian officials can be sure that every untaxed personal item is indeed leaving the country. Travelers should be sure to describe every item in exactly the same words on both arrival and departure, so that the customs official upon departure allows the goods to leave the country.

Where is my customs declaration?
Где моя таможенная декларация?
gd' yeh ma-YA ta-MO-zheh-na-ya deh-kla-RA-ts' ee-ya?

I do not have anything to declare.
Мне нечего предъявить.
mn' yeh N' YEH-cheh-va pr' yeh-d' ya-VEET.

These goods are personal.
Это личные вещи.
EH-ta LEECH-nee-yeh V' YEHSH-chee.

They are not for sale.
Они не продаются.
ah-NEE n' yeh pra-da-YOOT-sa.

Can you help me fill out this form?
Вы поможете мне заполнить этот бланк?
vee pa-MO-zhee-t' yeh mn' yeh zah-POL-neet EH-tot blahnk?

Precious metals and jewelry must be recorded on the customs form. Such personal items as rings, watches, cameras, and calculators may also need to be listed, depending upon the customs officer of the day. If the officer believes that a traveler intends to sell these items, they will be noted on the customs form, and they must then be brought out upon departure. Expensive business equipment – typewriters, computers, video equipment, tape recorders, fax machines, etc., will almost certainly be recorded on the customs form.

This is my own jewelry.

Это мои драгоценности.

EH-ta ma-yee dra-ga-TS'EH-nahs-tee.

This camera is for personal use only.

Эта камера только для личного пользования.

Eh-ta KA-meh-ra TOHL-ka dl'ya LEECH-na-va
POHL-za-va-nee-ya.

This calculator is not for sale.

Этот калькулятор не продается.

EH-taht kahl-koo-L'YA-tar n'yeh pra-da-YOHT-sa.

This equipment is for me to use on business.

Я буду употреблять это оборудование только для бизнеса.

yah BOO-do oo-po-tr'yeb-L'YAT EH-ta ah-ba-ROO-da-va-nee-yeh
TOHL-ka dl'ya BEEZ-neh-sa.

This is my own fax.

Это мой личный факс.

EH-ta moy LEECH-nee faks.

This is my own computer.

Это мой личный компьютер.

Eh-ta moy LEECH-nee kahm-P'YOO-ter.

I am not going to sell this.

Я этого не продам.

ya EH-ta-va n'yeh pra-DAM.

It is for my own use.

Это для моего личного пользования.

EH-ta dl'ya ma-ye-VO LEECH-na-va POHL-za-va-nee-ya.

Business samples may be brought into Russia with no duty charged, but it is probably helpful to have documentation that the samples have been requested by a Russian company. Otherwise, the traveler must convince the customs official that the samples are not for sale, but rather to demonstrate a product. The traveler without a letter from a Russian company requesting the samples faces two possible difficulties: being asked to pay duty on the samples upon entry, or being requested to account for them upon departure. Many Russian businesses send a representative to help foreign business travelers through customs on this account.

These are sample products.
Это образцы товаров.
EH-ta ahb-rahz-TS'EE ta-VA-rahf.

These products are not for sale.
Эти товары не продаются.
EH-tee ta-VA-ree n'yeh pra-da-YOOT-s'ya.

These samples were requested by a Russian company.
Эти образцы попрошены российской компанией.
EH-tee ahb-rahz-TS'EE pa-PRO-she-nee ra-SEE-skaee
kam-PA-nee-yey.

The .... company asked for these samples.
Компания .... попросила меня об этих образцах.
kahm-PA-nee-ya .... pa-pra-SEE-la m'yeh-n'YA ahb
EH-teekh ahb-rahz-TSAHKH.

Here is the letter requesting these samples.
Вот письмо, просящее эти образцы.
Voht pee-SMO, PRO-syah-shchee EH-tee ahb-rahz-TSEE.

A person from the company is meeting me here.
Человек из компании встречает меня здесь.
cheh-la-V'YEHK ees kahm-PA-nee-ee fstryeh-CHA-yeht
m'yeh-n'YA zdyehs.

Business travelers who are bringing in promotional or informational videotapes should make arrangements ahead of time with the companies they are visiting. If the host business provides the traveler with a letter taking responsibility for the video, the traveler will probably get through customs with little difficulty. Otherwise, customs officials will demand to see the video, causing unnecessary delay.

My hosts have requested this video.
Мои хозяева попросили это видео.
ma-EE kha-Z'YA-yeh-va pahp-ra-SEE-lee EH-ta video.

Here is the letter from my hosts.
Вот письмо от моих хозяев.
VOHT pee-SMO aht ma -EEKH kha -Z'YA -yehf.

The … Company will be responsible for this video.
Компания ... будет отвечать за это видео.
kahm-PA-nee-ya BOO-d'yeht aht-vyeh-CHANT za EH-ta video.

Some goods may not be brought into Russia under any circumstances. Pornography and anti-Russian literature are forbidden imports. So are roubles. Firearms or weapons may not be imported. Such goods as gold, antiques, and high-value electronics products may be brought in only if they are guaranteed to be re-exported.

I am taking my computer with me when I leave.
Я возьму свой компьютер со мной, когда я буду уезжать.
ya vahs-MOO svoy kahm-PYOO-ter sa mnoy kahg-DA ya BOO-doo oo-yehs-ZHANT.

I am taking this fax machine back to the United States.
Я возьму этот факс обратно в США.
ya vahs-MOO EH-tat fahx ahb-RAHT-na f'seh-sheh-AH.

There is a limit of one liter of alcohol or two liters of wine that may be imported duty-free, as well as 250 cigarettes and 250 grams of tobacco. The traveler carrying low-cost gifts for hosts – such as calculators, ties, fountain pens, watches, and audiocassette tapes – is not likely to be charged duty if there are fewer than ten of each item.

These are presents for my friends.
Это подарки для моих друзей.
EH-ta pa-DAHR-kee dl' ya ma-eekh drooz-YEY.

I am not selling these items; they are gifts!
Я не продам этого. Это подарки.
ya n' yeh pra-DAM EH-ta-va. EH-ta pa-DAR-kee.

This is all the liquor I have.
Это весь алкоголь, который у меня есть.
EH-ta v' yes ahl-ka-GOHL ka-TOH-ree oo m' yeh-N' YA yehst.

I have only one bottle of wine.
У меня только одна бутылка вина.
oo myeh-N' YA TOHL-ka ahd-NA boo-TEEL-ka vee-NA.

These are all the cigarettes I have.
Это все сигареты, которые у меня есть.
EH-ta fs' yeh see-ga-R' YEH-tee ka-TOH-ree-yeh oo m' yeh-N' YAH yehst.

I have less than 250 cigarettes!
У меня меньше двухсот пятидесяти сигарет.
oo myeh-NYA MYEHN-sheh dvookh-SOHT p' ya-TEE-d' yeh-s' yayh-tee see-ga-R' YEHT.

To make the customs process easier, Russians have instituted a two-tier system. Travelers with no valuables to declare may pass relatively quickly through the "green channel." Travelers with goods to declare must pass through the much slower "red channel." Any traveler carrying several pieces of luggage, or an unusually large amount of items that are scarce in Russia (such as electronic products, audiocassettes, film, cameras, video recorders, video cameras, jewelry, or books about Russia) will be directed to the red channel. The process of searching and examining luggage in the red channel can add another hour to the arrival process, as can the additional hour's wait for checked baggage.

Where is the green channel?
Где зеленый проход?
gd'yeh zee-L'YO-nee pra-HOD.

Have I filled out the form correctly?
Заполнил(а) ли я бланк правильно?
za-POHL-neel(ah) lee ya blahnk PRA-veel-na?

I only have carry-on luggage.
У меня только ручной багаж.
oo m'yeh-N'YA TOHL-ka rooch-NOY ba-GAHZH.

Where do I pick up my bags?
Где я получу свой багаж?
gd'yeh ya pa-loo-CHOO svoy ba-GAHZH.

When will the bags from Flight ………… be here?
Когда приедет багаж с полета …………?
kahg-DA pri-YEH-d'yeht ba -GAHZH ss pa -L'YOH-ta …………?

IMMUNIZATIONS

There are few immunizations required for visitors to Russia, although travelers to the Central Asian republics are recommended to have themselves immunized against tetanus, diphtheria, polio, and typhoid, as well as to receive gamma globulin. However, travelers arriving from South America or Africa must have a current International Certificate of Vaccination against yellow fever. Travelers coming from infected areas must also have a cholera vaccination certificate.

I have been vaccinated for yellow fever; here are the papers.
Мне привили желтую лихорадку. Вот документы.
mn'yeh pri-VI-li ZHOHL-too-yoo lee-kho-RAHD-koo.
Voht da-koo-M'YEHN-tee.

I have been vaccinated for cholera; here are the papers.
Мне привили холеру. Вот документы.
mn'yeh pree-VEE-lee kha-L'YEH-roo. Voht da-koo-M'YEHN-tee.

PASSPORTS AND VISAS

Of course, all visitors to Russia must have current passports. The Russians require that the passport remain valid for at least three months beyond the planned date of departure from Russia.

Here is my passport.
Вот мой паспорт.
voht moy PAHS-port.

My passport will be valid for another six months.
Мой паспорт действителен еще на шесть месяцев.
moy PAHS-port dey-STVEE-t' yeh-l' yehn yehsh-CHO nah shehst M' YEH-syah-tsehf.

My passport is valid for several more years.
Мой паспорт действителен еще на несколько лет.
moy PAHS-port dey-STVEE-t' yeh-l' yehn yi-SH' CHO na N' YEHS-kahl-ka L' YEHT.

In addition to a passport, a visa is required. Transit visas are good for three days – sufficient for the traveler en route to another destination. Tourist visas are readily available, but the business traveler will find that official sponsorship makes a trip far easier. Official sponsorship usually produces an ordinary visa, although sometimes a multiple visa – good for two or more visits – is available to business people, scientists, or technicians who travel frequently to Russia.

Here is my visa.
Вот моя виза.
voht ma-YA visa.

I have a tourist visa.
У меня туристическая виза.
oo m' yeh-N' YA too-rees-TEE-ch' yehs-ka-ya visa.

I am a business traveler.
Я езжу по бизнесу.
ya YEH-zhoo pa BEE-zn' yeh-soo.

.... is sponsoring me.
.... **субсидирует меня.**
.... *soop-see-DEE-roo-yeht meh-N'YA.*

A Russian visa comes in sections, one of which is given up to the immigration authorities upon arrival, the rest of which are taken upon departure. There is thus no record in a traveler's passport of a stay in Russia.

Visas list exact destinations and departure times. Any changes in itinerary and any extensions of stay must be approved, although usually this is not difficult, particularly if the traveler has reserved additional hotel nights and is willing to pay for them in hard currency. The hotel service that makes the reservation will usually handle the visa extension as well.

Can you extend my visa?
Можете ли вы продлить мою визу?
MO-zhee-t' yeh lee vee prahd-LEET ma-YOO VEE-zoo.

I want to leave on ....
Я хочу уехать ....
ya kha-CHOO oo-YEH-khaht ....

I want to travel to ....
Я хочу поехать в ....
ya kha-CHOO pa-YEH-KHAHT v' ....

This visa has been extended.
Эта виза продлена.
EH-ta VEE-za prahd-l' yeh-NA.

GENERAL PHRASES
Memorize these expressions for high-frequency use.

Please
Пожалуйста............
pa -ZHAHL-sta ....

Thank you
Спасибо
spa -SEE-ba.

One moment
Минуточку
mee-NOO-tahch-koo.

Where is my luggage?
Где мой багаж?
gd' yeh moy ba-GAHZH.

Is that all?
Это все?
EH-ta fs' yo?

Where do I go now?
Куда идти теперь?
koo-DA ee-TEE t' yeh-P' YEHR?

AT THE HOTEL

4

Most business travelers find it easier to travel as invited guests of particular Russian organizations or enterprises, in which case they will probably be met at the airport by their hosts. If they are not met at the airport, most business travelers will want to proceed directly to their hotels as soon as they have passed through customs.

TAXIS FROM THE AIRPORT

The simplest way of reaching one's hotel is usually by taxi. There are some official taxis in Russia. In addition, many owners of cars pick up passengers for pay.

Can you take me to my hotel?
Можете ли вы довезти меня до моего отеля?
MO-zhet-yeh lee vwee da-v'yes-TEE men-YA da ma-yeh-VO o-TEL-ya?

I am staying at ....
Я сейчас проживаю в ....
ya sey-CHAHS pra-zhee-VAY-yoo v ....

Most taxi drivers do not speak English, so a traveler may have to ask someone to give instructions to the driver.

Do you speak English?
Говорите ли вы по-английски?
ga-va-REE-t'yeh lee vwee pa ahn-GLEE-skee?

Please tell the driver to take me to the hotel ....
Пожалуйста, скажите водителю отвезти меня в Отель ....
pa-ZHAL-sta ska-ZHEE-t'yeh vo-DEE-t'yel-yoo aht-ves-tee men-ya v'o-t'YEL' ....

Taxi! To the hotel ...., please.
Такси! В отель ...., пожалуйста.
TAK-see! v' o-t'YEL' ...., pa-ZHAHL-sta.

Official taxis are usually yellow with a checkered design on their doors and a small green light on the upper right-hand corner of the windshield. Theoretically, when this light is on, the taxi is free.

However, a taxi may not stop for a traveler. If a taxi does stop, the driver may first ask where a traveler is headed and then ask how much he or she is willing to pay.

Where are you going?
Куда вы едете?
koo-DA vwee YEH-deh-t' yeh?

How much?
Сколько стоит?
SKOHL-ka STO-yeet?

Excuse me, I do not speak Russian.
Простите меня, я не говорю по-русски.
pra-STEE-t' yeh MEN-ya, ya n' yeh ga-va-R'YOO pa ROO-skee.

The address is on this paper.
Адрес на этой бумажке.
ah-DRESS na EH-toy boo-MAZH-keh.

Official taxis are supposed to use their meters but rarely do. Instead, they are likely to charge from seven to ten times higher than the official fare, which is 20 kopeks (about 3 cents) per kilometer, plus tip. Unofficial taxis or private cars rely almost exclusively on bargaining ahead of time, at least for foreign passengers.

How much will you charge me?
Сколько это мне будет стоить?
SKOHL-ka EH-ta m' nyeh BOO-d' yet STO-yeet?

That's too much!
Это слишком много!
EH-ta SLISH-kom MNO-ga!

I'll give you this much.
Я вам дам вот столько.
ya vahm dahm vot STOHL'-ka.

Frequently, Soviets share cabs with each other, even with strangers.

Foreign travelers are advised to make every effort to share a cab with a Soviet, who may be able to get the driver to use the meter, or at least to negotiate a reasonable fare. Metered fares should be supplemented with a tip; privately agreed-on fares *are* a tip and do not need to be supplemented. Some taxi drivers will accept a carton of cigarettes in lieu of money. Many drivers will insist on payment in foreign currency, which is illegal; business travelers should insist in turn on paying in roubles but many taxi drivers will not take roubles under any circumstances.

Would you like to share this cab?
Вы бы хотели поехать вместе на этом такси?
vwee bee ha-T'YEH-lee pa-YEH-haht' v'M'YES-teh na EH-tom tak-SEE?

Please tell the taxi driver to take me to this address.
Пожалуйста, скажите водителю отвезти меня на этот адрес.
pa-ZHAHL-sta ska-ZHEE-t'yeh va-dee-t'YEL-yoo aht-ves-TEE men-YA na EH-toht AH-dress.

How much will he charge?
Сколько он от нас потребует?
SKOHL-ka ohn aht nahss pa-TR'YEH-boo-yit?

Is that a fair price?
Это хорошая цена?
EH-ta ha-RO-sha-ya tseh-NA?

Will you accept these cigarettes instead?
Возьмете ли вы в оплату эти сигареты?
vohz-MYOH-t'yeh lee vwee v ahp-LA-too EH-tee see-ga-REH-tee?

Even though most cab drivers do not speak English, they may still try to converse with their foreign passengers. They may also try to prevent passengers from fastening their seat belts, viewing the use of safety devices as an insult to their driving. Foreign visitors should nonetheless take every precaution, particularly in winter when roads are icy and many cars do not have snow tires.

RESERVING A ROOM

Once travelers arrive at their hotels, they are likely to find at least some employees who speak English. The range of fluency, however, is likely to vary. Soviet tourist agencies have been keen to increase tourism, and many partnerships with foreign firms have been established to build or upgrade new hotels. However, the influx of tourism coincided with crises in the Soviet economy, so that many luxury hotels are closed for renovation or still under construction. Tour groups tend to take priority over individual travelers, and business travelers should in any case be prepared for standards that may not be up to Western levels.

The traveler who has not made a reservation through a foreign tourist agency will almost certainly be staying at a municipal hotel, rather than a luxury one. Staff in these establishments are far less likely to speak English. Even luxury hotel reservations may not come through to a traveler's satisfaction, although requesting a deluxe room or suite increases a visitor's chances of getting into the hotel of his or her choice.

I have a reservation.
У меня забронирован номер в отеле.
oo men-YA za-pra-NEE-ro-vahn NO-mer v' o-T'YEH-leh.

I want a single room.
Я хочу номер на одного.
ya ha-CHOO NO-myer na ahd-na-VO.

I want a deluxe room.
Я хочу номер делюкс.
ya ha-CHOO NO-mer deh-L'YOOX.

I want a suite.
Я хочу номер свит.
ya ha-CHOO NO-mer sveet.

What are your rates?
Какие у вас расценки?
ka-KEE-yeh oo vahs ra-TSEN-kee.

Business travelers staying in Moscow may apply for rooms at the Mezhdunarodnaya ("International") Hotel, which is run by Sovincentr for those traveling on business visas.

I have a business visa.
У меня есть бизнес-виза.
oo MEN-ya yest BIZ-ness VEE-za.

My reservation has been confirmed.
Моя броня была подтверждена.
ma-YA BRO-nya bee-LA pohd-tverzh-d' yeh-NA.

Travelers should also be aware that in summer, from two weeks, to three months' notice may be necessary to reserve rooms in cities that are popular with tourists.

Russian hotels have three rankings: deluxe, first-class, or tourist. In practice, first-class and deluxe hotels are often indistinguishable. These categories are not very reliable, since Intourist (the Russian tourist agency) determines its ratings on a purely objective basis – number of restaurants, room size, etc. – ignoring such elements of luxury and comfort as style of furnishings, landscaping, and age of building. However, the standard of many Russian/Western joint venture hotel is now equivalent to good four or five star Western hotels.

First-class rooms should include a portable color television set, piped radio, and a bathroom with sink, tub, shower attachment, toilet, and heated towel rail, in addition to single or twin beds and a small wall-mounted desk. Central heating is included with first-class rooms, but air-conditioning frequently is not.

Does this room have air-conditioning?
Есть ли кондиционер в этом номере?
yesst lee kohn-deets-yo-NAIR v' EH-tohm NO-meh-reh?

Can I get an air-conditioned room?
Могу ли я получить номер с кондиционером?
*ma-GOO lee ya pa-l' yoo-CHEET' NO-mer
s' kohn-dee-ts' yohn-NEH-rahm?*

Is there an electric fan?
Есть ли вентилятор?
yesst' lee vehn-tee-L'YA-tor?

A two-room suite will further include a living room, work desk, refrigerator, and a larger television set – plus air-conditioning. A three-room suite has the advantage of a study, as well, with perhaps a second bathroom or a dressing room.

I would like a two-room suite.
Я бы хотел (хотела) двухкомнатный номер свит.
ya bwee ha-T'YEL (ha-T'YEL-a) DVUH-kohm-naht-nee NO-mer sveet.

Does this room have a refrigerator?
Есть ли холодильник в этом номере?
YEST' lee ha-LO-deel'nik v' EH-tahm NO-meh-reh?

How many bathrooms are included?
Сколько ванных и туалетов там есть?
SKOHL-ka VAHN-nikh ee t'ya-L'YEH-tahv tahm yehst?

CHECKING IN

Checking into a hotel generally means presenting an Intourist voucher, unless other payment arrangements have been made. It is customary for Russian hotels to take a visitor's passport and keep it at the reception desk, sometimes for a day only, sometimes for longer. A *propusk*, or hotel pass, will be issued to each resident. Hotels generally ask to see *propusks* before allowing guests to enter, particularly at luxury hotels or hotels with many foreigners, to keep black marketeers and petty criminals from preying on guests with hard currency.

Here is my passport.
Вот мой паспорт.
voht moy PAS-port.

When can I have my passport back?
Когда я могу получить свой паспорт назад?
kahg-DA ya ma-GHOO pa-loo-CHEET' svoy PAS-port na-ZAHD?

Here is my hotel pass.
Это мой пропуск в отель.
EH-to moy pro-POOSK v' o-T'YEL.

I am a guest here.
Я здесь гость.
ya zd'yess gohst'.

ROOMS AND FACILITIES

Television and radio in Russian hotels are usually all in Russian. Exercise or music programs may interest some foreign travelers. Some hotels offer a promotional channel that shows tourist films in English.

Is there an English channel on this T.V.?
Есть ли на этом телевизоре канал на английском языке?
yest' lee nah EH-tahm teh-leh-VEE-zo-reh ka-NAL na ahn-GLEE-skom ya-zee-K'YEH?

Beds in Russian hotels are usually made every day, but the linen is generally changed only once a week. In older hotels, the attendant unmakes the bed in the morning and folds the linen neatly, leaving travelers to remake their own beds in the evening.

Usually only two old, worn towels per person are allowed. While baths generally have shower attachments, they may not have shower curtains or plugs (travelers who enjoy baths or who want to wash out clothes in the sink are advised to bring flat rubber stoppers that will fit over any drain).

Can I have more towels, please?
Можно ли мне иметь дополнительные полотенца, пожалуйста?
MOZH-na lee mn'yeh eem-YET' da-pahl-NEE-t'yehl-nee-yeh pa-la-TEN-t'sa, pa-ZHAHL-sta?

Is there a plug for this bathtub?
Есть ли пробка от этой ванны?
yest' lee PROHB-ka oht EH-toy VAHN-nee?

FOOD AND DRINK

Hotel restaurants generally offer good food at reasonable prices, although service tends to be far below Western standards and patience and diplomacy are usually necessary. There is usually more than one restaurant available at a good hotel, but reservations are definitely necessary in advance.

Where are the restaurants in this hotel?
Где рестораны в этом отеле?
gd'yeh res-ta-RA-nee v' EH-tom o-TEL'-yeh?

I want to make a reservation for dinner.
Я бы хотел (хотела) заказать стол на ужин.
ya bee ha-T'YEL (ha-T'YEL-a) za-ka-ZAHT stohl na OO-zhen.

There will be .... people in our party.
В нашей компании будет .... человек.
v' NA-shey kom-PA-nee BOOD-yet .... cheh-lo-VEK.

Do you have an English menu?
Есть ли у вас меню на английском языке?
yest lee oo vahss mehn-YOO na ahn-GLEE-skohm ya-zee-K'YEH?

What time do you serve breakfast?
В какое время завтрак?
v'ka-KO-yeh VREM-ya ZAFT-rahk?

When do you serve lunch?
В какое время обед?
v'ka-KO-yeh VREM-ya ahb-YED?

What time does dinner service begin?
В какое время вы начинаете подавать ужин?
v'ka-KO-yeh VREM-ya vwee na-chee-NA-yet-yeh pa-da-VAHT' OO-zhin?

How late do you serve dinner?
До какого времени бы подаете ужин?
da ka-KO-va VREH-meh-nee vwee pa-da-YOT-yeh OO-zhin?

Bars in Russian hotels may serve only crackers, or they may serve light snacks that tend to run out by mid-evening. Usually, most hotel establishments close at 11 p.m., except for one bar that may stay open as late as 4 a.m.

How late are you open?
До какого времени вы открыты?
da ka-KO-va VREH-meh-nee vwee aht-KRYEE-tee?

Is there a bar or restaurant that is still open?
Есть ли бар или ресторан, который ещё открыт?
yest lee bar EE-lee res-to-RAHN, ka-TOH-ree yesh-CHO aht-KREET?

I haven't eaten yet.
Я ещё не ел (ела).
ya yesh-CHO n'yeh yell (yella)

Can I still order food?
Могу ли я все ещё заказать поесть?
ma-GOO lee ya fs'yo yish-CHO za-ka-ZAHT' pa-YEST'?

SERVICE DESK

Hotels are set up differently in Russia, depending on their age. The older hotels usually have a service counter on each floor, run by the *dezhurnaya*, or female attendant. The dezhurnaya keeps each traveler's key, provides tea, holds mail, passes on messages, and bars unwelcome or questionable people from entry onto the floor. Some dezhurnayas call taxis or help with placing international calls. Room service – other than tea – is almost never available (although some hotels claim otherwise!).

Where is the service desk, please?
Где стол обслуживания?
gd'yeh stohl ahb-SLOOZH-ee-va-n'ya?

Hello! It's nice to meet you!
Здравствуйте, очень приятно с вами встретиться!
ZDRAHST-vwee-tyeh, O-chen' pree-YAHT-na s'VA-mee vst-reh-TEET'-s'ya!

My name is ....
Меня зовут ....
MEN-ya za-VOOT ....

I am in room ....
Я в номере ....
ya v' NO-meh-reh ....

I would like to order tea.
Я бы хотел (хотела) заказать чаю.
ya bih ha-T'YEL (ha-T'YEL-a) za-ka-ZAHT' CHA-yoo.

I would like to order some drinks.
Я бы хотел (хотела) заказать напитки.
ya bih ha-T'YEL (ha-T'YEL-a) za-ka-ZAHT na-PEET-kee.

I would like to order some food.
Я бы хотел (хотела) заказать еду.
ya bih ha-T'YEL (ha-T'YEL-a) za-ka-ZAHT YEH-doo.

Can you help me to make a telephone call?
Можете ли вы помочь мне позвонить по телефону?
MO-zheh-t' yeh lee vwee pa-MOTCH' mn' yeh pa-zva-NEET pa teh-leh-FO-noo?

I am waiting for an important call.
Я ожидаю важныи разговор.
ya o-zhee-DA-yoo VAHZH-nee rahz-ga-VOHR.

Are there any messages for me?
Были ли для меня телефонные сообщения?
BIL-yee lee dl' ya men-YA teh-leh-FO-nee-yeh sa-ahbsh-CHEH-nee-ya?

Did I get any mail?
Получил (Получила) ли я почту?
pa-loo-CHEEL (pa-loo-CHEEL-a) lee ya POHCH-too?

Can you get me a taxi?
Можети ли вы достать мне такси?
MO-zheh-tee lee vwee da-STAHT' mn-yeh tak-SEE?

In both older and newer hotels, the hotel service desk is available to
help the traveler with just about every other service. Theater and concert tickets, dinner reservations, travel arrangements, car rentals, guid-
ed tours, use of sports facilities, extension of a hotel stay, and extension of a visa can all be obtained through a hotel service desk.

I'd like to order theater tickets please.
Я бы хотел (хотела) достать билеты в театр, пожалуйста.
*ya bwee ha-T'YEL (ha-T'YEL-a) da-STAHT' beel-YEHT-tee v'
teh-AH-ter, pa-ZAHL-sta.*

What plays are available tonight?
На какие спектакли сегодня вечером есть билеты?
*na ka-KEE-yeh spek-TA-klee seh-VO-d'nya VETCH-er-rohm yest'
beel-YEH-tee?*

What is playing this week?
Что идет на этой неделе?
ch'toh ee-D'YOHT na eh-TOY n'yeh-DEH-l'yeh?

Can I get concert tickets here?
Могу ли я здесь достать билеты на концерт?
ma-GOO lee ya zdyess da-STAHT beel-YEH-tee na kon-TSERT?

Will you make a dinner reservation for me, please?
**Можете ли вы заказать столик на ужин для меня,
пожалуйста?**
*MO-zheh-tee lee vwee za-ka-ZAHT' STO-leek na OO-zhin
dl'ya men-YA, pa-ZHAHL-sta?*

What restaurant do you recommend?
Какой ресторан вы рекомендуете?
ka-KOY res-ta-RAHN vwee reh-ko-men-DOO-yet-yeh?

AT THE HOTEL

I need help making travel arrangements.
Мне нужна помощь в организации моего путешествия.
*mn'yeh noozh-NA PO-mash'ch v ar-ga-nee-ZAHT-tsee-yee
ma-yeh-VOH poo-teh-SHEST-vee-ya.*

This is where I want to go.
Вот сюда я хочу ехать.
voht s'yoo-DA ya ha-CHOO YEH-haht'.

I want to go by plane.
Я хочу ехать на самолёте.
ya ha-CHOO YEH-haht' na sa-mahl-YO-teh.

I want to go by train.
Я хочу ехать поездом.
ya ha-CHOO YEH-haht' PO-yiz-dahm.

Where is the schedule?
Где расписание?
gd'yeh ra-spee-SA-nee-yeh?

I need to stay here longer.
Мне нужно остаться здесь дольше.
mn'yeh NOOZH-na ah-STA-ts'ya zdyess' DOHL'-sheh.

I need to extend my visa.
Мне нужно продлить мою визу.
mn'yeh NOOZH-na pro-D'LEET' ma-YOO VEE-zoo.

Who can help me with this?
Кто мне с этим может помочь?
kto mn'yeh s EH-tim MO-zhet pa-MOH'CH'?

Where do I go?
Куда мне идти?
koo-DA mn'yeh eed-TEE?

Service counters may also be able to help tourists with laundry service, placing international telephone calls, medical assistance, reading Russian addresses, and a host of other problems.

Can I leave my laundry with you?
Можно ли мне дать вам моё грязное бельё для стирки?
MOHZH-na lee mn'yeh daht' vahm ma-YO GR'YAZ-na-yeh byil-YO dl'ya STEER-kee?

When will it be ready?
Когда оно будет готово?
kahg-DA ah-NO BOOD-yet ga-TOH-va?

Travelers are well advised to be patient with Russian service personnel. Western tourists usually want services to be performed quickly and to specification; Russians move much more slowly and with a sense that their own needs are as important as those of the customers they are serving. However, if they are courteous and persistent, Western tourists will find Russian service people friendly, helpful, and hospitable.

You speak excellent English.
Вы говорите прекрасно по-английски.
vwee ga-va-REET-yeh preh-KRA-sna pa ahn-GLEE-skee.

Thanks for your help!
Спасибо за вашу помошь!
spa-SEE-ba za VA-shoo PO-mashch!

You are very kind.
Вы очень добры.
vwee O-chen' DOH-bree.

BUSINESS SERVICES

Russian hotels tend not to have the kinds of facilities that business travelers need – faxes, computer services, even typewriters. Most hotels can provide a telex bureau. Intourist provides interpreters for tourists, but business travelers may also find some help there. However, the Mezhdunarodnaya Hotel in Moscow does offer a range of business services.

Do you have a fax machine?
Есть ли у вас факс?
yesst lee oo vahss fahx?

Do you have a telex?
Есть ли у вас телекс?
yesst lee oo vahss T'YEH'-lex?

Do you have an English typewriter?
Есть ли у вас пишущая машинка на английском языке?
yesst lee oo vahss PEE-shosh-cha-ya ma-SHEEN-ka na
ahn-GLEE-skom ya-zee-KYEH?

Where can I hire an interpreter?
Где могу ли я нанимать переводчика?
gd'yeh ma-GOO lee ya na-nee-MAHT' pyeh-ryeh-VOHD-chik-a?

TELEPHONES, TELEXES, TELEGRAMS, AND MAIL

5

Most business travelers to Russia are extremely frustrated with the phone service there, which poses difficulties for both incoming and outgoing calls. Each hotel room has its own telephone number. Thus, incoming calls come directly to the traveler's room – and, if the traveler isn't there, no one else is available to take a message. The number of the hotel room is usually printed on the room's phone; or it may be listed in a directory giving the phone number for every room in the hotel.

TELEPHONES

What is the telephone number of my hotel room?

Телефонный номер моего номера в гостинице какой?

t' yee-lee-FOHN-nee NO-m' yehr
mah-yee-VO NO-m' yeh-ra vga-STEE-nee-tseh ka-koy?

Is there a telephone directory for this hotel?

Есть ли телефонный справочник для этой гостиницы?

YEHST lee t' yee-lee-FOHN-nee SPRA-votch-nick dl' ya
EH-ta-ee ga-STEE-nee-tsee?

I'm trying to contact (Mr.) (Mrs.) (Miss) .... in Room ....

Я хочу разговаривать с (господином) (госпожой) ....
в номере ....

Ya ha-CHOO ras-ga-VA-ree-vat ss (ga-spa-DEE-nam)
(ga-spa-ZHOY) .... VNO-m' yeh-r' yeh ....

Local outgoing calls can usually be made directly from the hotel room phone, although sometimes the traveler must dial "9" or "0" first. Travelers can also use pay phone booths located throughout the city, but these are unreliable at best. These calls cost 20 kopeks for the first few minutes, with additional coins accepted after the operator warns that time is running out. Phones will accept 20-kopek and 1-rouble pieces. Sometimes it takes a while to get a dial tone on Russian pay phones; occasionally, after making two or three calls, a person may be interrupted by a busy signal and must then try to get the dial tone again. In Moscow and Leningrad, people must deposit their coins before picking up the receiver and dialing.

TELEPHONES, TELEXES, TELEGRAMS, AND MAIL

How do I dial an outside number on this phone?
Как я набираю номер вне гостиницы с этого телефона?
KAHK ya na-bee-RA-'yoo NO-m'yer vn'yeh ga-STEE-nee-tsee ss EH-ta-va teh-leh-FO-na?

Do I have to dial (0) (9)?
Надо мне набрать (ноль) (девять)?
NA-da mn'yeh nah-BRAHT (nol) (D'YEH-v'yat)?

Where can I make a phone call?
Где я могу позвонить?
gd'yeh ya ma-GOO pa-zva-NEET?

Where can I get change?
Где я могу получить мелочь?
gd'yeh ya ma-GOO pa-loo-CHIT M'YEH-lahch?

Can you give me change?
Вы можете мне дать мелочь?
vee MO-zhee-t'yeh mn'yeh daht M'YEH-lahch?

I need some 20-kopek pieces for the phone.
Мне нужно несколько двадцатикопеечных для телефона.
mn'yeh NOO-zhna N'YEH-skal-ka DVA-tsaht-ee-ka-P'YEH-yehch-neekh dl'ya teh-leh-FO-na.

Long-distance and international calls may be made from the traveler's hotel. In Moscow, travelers must phone the long-distance operator themselves. Elsewhere, they may reserve their calls through the hotel service bureau, or through the *dezhurhnaya* on their floor.

I want to make a long-distance call.
Я хочу вести международный разговор.
ya kha-CHOO vyeh-STEE m'yeh-zhdoo-na-ROD-nee rahz-ga-VOHR.

to the USA.
в США.
f'ss-SHA.

to France.
во Францию.
va FRAHN-tsee-yoo.

to England.
в Англию.
b AHN-glee-'yoo.

to Germany.
в Германию.
v g'yer-MA-nee-yoo.

to Japan.
в Японию.
v ya-PO-nee-'yoo

to Switzerland.
в Швейцарию.
f'shvey-TSA-ree-'yoo.

to Canada.
в Канаду.
f'ka-NA-doo.

to South America.
в Южную Америку.
v 'YOOZH-noo-'yoo ah-M'YEH-ree-koo.

Can you make an international call for me?
Вы можете установить международный разговор для меня?
vee MO-zhee-t'yeh oo-sta-na-VEET
m'yeh-zhdoo-na-ROD-nee rahz-ga-VOHR dl'ya m'yeh-N'YA?

Where do I place an overseas call?
Где я могу установить международный разговор?
gd'yeh ya ma-GOO oo-sta-na-VEET
m'yeh-zhdoo-na-ROD-nee rahz-ga-VOHR?

Travelers may have to wait at least an hour before their long-distance calls go through; the operator will call back to let them know that an overseas line is now free. Both hotel operators and telephone operators are likely to answer in Russian, so travelers should be prepared to ask for one who speaks English.

Excuse me, do you speak English?

Извините, вы говорите по-английски?

eez-vee-NEE-t' yeh, vee ga-va-REE-t' yeh pa-an-GLEE-skee?

How long must I wait?

Как долго я должен (должна) ждать?

KAHK DOL-ga ya DOL-zhen (dahl-ZHNAH) ZHDAT?

It is very urgent.

Это очень срочно.

EH-ta OH-ch' yen SRO-chna.

Sometimes a long-distance call will be cut off in mid-conversation. The operator may call back to see whether the call has been completed and to reconnect, or the traveler may have to find the operator and start again.

My call has been cut off.

Мой разговор прервался.

moy rahz-ga-VOR prehr-VAHL-s' ya.

Can you reconnect me?

Вы можете соединить меня снова?

vee MO-zhee-t' yeh sa-' yeh-dee-NEET' m' yeh-n' ya SNO-va?

Hotels have different policies about when to pay for long-distance calls. Sometimes payment is required immediately; at other times, the traveler may wait until the next time he or she picks up the room key. In either case, payment must be in hard currency or by credit card. There are not yet any collect calls from Russia.

Where do I pay for this call?

Где я плачу за этот разговор?

gd' yeh ya pla-CHOO za EH-tat rahz-ga-VOR?

When must I pay?
Когда я должен (должна) платить?
kahg-DA ya DOHL-zhen (dahl-ZHNA) pla-TEET?

How much did my call cost?
Сколько стоил мой разговор?
SKOL-ka STO-eel moy rahz-ga-VOR?

Generally, long-distance phone calls are of poor quality. Experienced travelers recommend not discussing confidential matters during any phone call, local or long distance.

By the way, there are no telephone directories in Russia, so it's a good idea to save all business cards carefully and to ask for phone numbers when presented with a card. It may even be easier to get the correct phone numbers from the traveler's home country than from Russia itself.

Can you give me your telephone number?
Вы можете дать мне свой номер телефона?
vee MO-zhee-t' yeh daht mn' yeh svoy NO-m' yehr teh-leh-FO-na?

Is your number on this card?
Ваш номер на этой карточке?
vash NO-m' yehr na EH-ta-ee KAR-tohch-keh?

It isn't easy getting people to take messages in Russia. If a call is answered but the person the traveler wants to speak to isn't there, the person who answered may just hang up. Having a Russian speaker make the phone call may increase the traveler's chance of getting a message taken.

Can I speak with (Mr.) (Mrs.) (Miss) ....?
Могу я говортиь с (господином) (госпожой) ....?
ma-GOO ya ga-va-REET ss (ga-spa-DEE-nahm) (ga-spa-ZHOY) ....?

Can you call him (her) to the phone?
Вы можете позвать его (ее) к телефону?
vee MO-zhee-t' yeh pahz-VAHT yeh-VO (yeh-YO) k't' yeh-li-FO-noo?

May I leave a message?
Могу я оставить записку?
ma-GOO ya as-TA-veet za-PEE-skoo?

It's very important.
Это очень важно.
EH-ta OH-ch' yen VA-zhna.

Thank you very much.
Большое спасибо.
bal-SHO-' yeh spa-SEE-ba.

TELEXES

Telexes are rare in Russia. The Intourist Hotel and the Mezhdunarodnaya Hotel in Moscow do have public telex facilities. Otherwise, particularly outside Moscow, the business traveler will probably have to send telexes from the local post office. There will certainly be several forms to fill out, and the assistance of an interpreter will almost certainly be necessary.

Where can I send a telex?
Где я могу послать телекс?
gd' yeh ya ma-GOO pahs-LAT T' YEH-l' yehks?

Here is the number.
Вот номер.
voht NO-m' yehr.

Here is the text.
Вот текст.
voht t' yext.

How much will it cost?
Сколько это будет стоить?
SKOHL-ka EH-ta BOO-d' yeht STO-eet?

Can you help me with this form?
Вы можете мне помочь с этим бланком?
vee MO-zhee-t' yeh mn' yeh pa-MOCH SEH-teem BLAHNK-ahm?

Thanks for your help.
Спасибо за вашу помощь.
spa-SEE-ba za BA-shoo PO-mashch.

TELEGRAMS

On the whole, telegrams are probably more reliable than phone service for long-distance communication. Travelers might check with their hotels about telegram facilities, but once again, particularly outside Moscow, the local post office may be the best choice.

May I send a telegram?
Могу я послать телеграмму?
ma-GOO ya pahs-LAHT t'yeh-l'yeh-GRA-moo?

When will it arrive?
Когда она придет?
kahk-DA ah-NA pree-D'YOT?

It is urgent.
Это срочно.
EH-ta SRO-ch'na.

Does this hotel have a telegraph office?
В этой гостинице есть телеграф?
v'EH-tay gas-TEE-nee-tseh yehst t'yeh-l'yeh-GRAF?

When is it open?
Когда он открыт?
kahk-DA OHN aht-KREET?

How do I get to the post office?
Как я попаду на почту?
KAHK ya pa-pa-DOO na POCH-too?

What are its opening hours?
Какие ее часы работы?
ka-KEE-y'eh yeh-YO cha-SEE ra-bo-TEE?

MAIL

All hotels where tourists are likely to stay will have their own post offices for stamps, air mail, and small packages. To send larger packages, the business traveler will have to go to a city post office, preferably with an unwrapped package. After inspection, the postal staff will do the wrapping, after selling the traveler the appropriate box. As with any international dealings, sending packages overseas requires the filling out of forms.

Where is the hotel post office?
Где почта в гостинице?
gdy' eh POHCH-ta f gas-TEE-nee-tseh?

Can I mail this from here?
Могу я отправить это отсюда?
ma-GOO ya aht-PRA-veet EH-ta aht-SY' oo-da?

Can you wrap this for me?
Вы можете упаковать это для меня?
vee MO-zheh-ty' eh oo-pa-ka-VAHT EH-ta dly' a meh-NY' A?

How much will it cost?
Сколько это стоит?
SKOHL-ka EH-ta STO-eet?

Where can I mail a letter?
Где я могу отправить письмо?
gdy' eh ya ma-GOO aht-PRA-veet pees-MO?

I want to send a package.
Я хочу отправить посылку.
ya kha-CHOO aht-PRA-veet pa-SEEL-koo.

Can you help me fill out this form?
Вы можете мне помочь заполнить этот бланк?
vee MO-zhee-t' yeh mn' yeh pa-MOHCH za-POHL-neet EH-tot blahnk?

A new U.S.–Russian pact has improved the speed of mail service between those two countries. Express Mail International Service (EMIS) is therefore available between Moscow and the United States.

If a letter arrives in Moscow before 5:00 a.m., it will reach the United States that day; otherwise it will arrive the following day, except when offices are closed for weekends and holidays. Within Russia, however, and even within Moscow, mail service is slow and unpredictable. Many Russian businesses prefer messenger services for sending material within the same city. Russian–Europe air mail generally takes about 10 days.

Can I send this EMIS?
Могу я послать это по Международной Службе Почты Экспресс?
ma-GOO ya pahs-LAHT EH-ta pa mehzh-doo-na-ROHD-na-ee SLOOZH-beh POCH-tee ex-PRESS?

When will this letter reach the United States?
Когда это письмо придет в Соединенные Штаты?
kahk-DA EH-ta pees-MO pree-D'YOHT v sa-yi-di-N'YOHN-nee-yeh SHTA-tee?

Can I send this by messenger?
Могу я послать это с посыльным?
ma-GOO ya pahs-LAHT EH-ta ss'pa-SEEL-neem?

Can you help me call a messenger service?
Вы можете мне помочь позвонить посыльной службе?
vee MO-zheh-t'yeh mn'yeh pa-MOHCH pa-zva-NEET pa-SEEL-noy SLOOZH-b'yeh?

COURIERS
Courier service for materials, parts, or samples is available in Moscow and Leningrad at the offices of international airlines. Federal Express and DHL Worldwide Express also offer a courier service for small parcels.

How do I reach Federal Express?
Как я могу достигнуть Федерал Экспресс?
Kahk ya ma-GOO dah-STIG-noot FEderal exPRESS?

Where can I call DHL?
Где я могу позвонить ДиЭйчЭл?
gd'yeh ya ma-GOO pahz-va-NEET DHL?

SETTING UP A
BUSINESS MEETING

6

INTRODUCTIONS

Frequently, as previously mentioned, business travelers will have managed to receive an official invitation from some Russian organization or enterprise. In this case, the host organization will probably send officials to meet their guests at the airport upon arrival – or, at the very least, will send a car and driver.

Thank you for meeting me.
Спасибо за встречу.
spa-SEE-ba za fst-R'YEH-choo.

I am happy to meet you.
Счастлив (счастлива) познакомиться с вами.
S'CHA-stleef (S'CHA-stlee-va) pa-zna-KO-mee-tsa s'VA-mee.

Thanks for sending the car.
Спасибо за отравление машины.
spa-SEE-ba-za aht-pra-VL'YEH-nee-yeh ma-SHEE-nee.

I arrived at my hotel with no problems, thank you!
Я прибыл (прибыла) в гостиницу без проблем, спасибо!
ya PREE-beel (pree-be-LA) f' gahs-TEE-nee-tsoo b'yehz pra-BL'YEHM, spa-SEE-ba!

Like many Europeans, the Russians value continuity in a business relationship. To the greatest extent possible, then, a company will benefit from continuing to send the same negotiators to Russia.

I was here last year.
Я был (была) здесь в прошлом году.
ya beel (bee-LA) zd'yes f'PROHSH-lahm ga-DOO.

I met with your company last month.
Я посетил (посетила) вашу компанию в прошлом месяце.
ya pa-s'yeh-TEEL (pa-s'ye-TEE-la) VA-shoo kahm-PA-nee-yoo f PROHSH-lahm M'YEH-s'ya-tseh.

(NB: words in parenthesis indicate the feminine form of the noun, verb or adjective.)

SETTING UP A MEETING

I work with (Mr./Ms.) ....
Я работаю с (господином/госпожой) ....
ya ra-BO-ta-yoo ss' (ga-spa-DEE-nahm/ga-spa-ZHOY) ....

Last time I spoke with (Mr./Ms.) ....
**В последнии раз я разговаривал (разговаривала) с
(господином/госпожой)** ....
*f pahs-LY'EH-dnee RAHS ya rahz-ga-VA-ree-vahl
(rahz-ga-VA-ree-va-la) ss
(ga-spa-DEE-nahm/ga-spa-ZHOY)* ....

I am a friend of (Mr./Ms.) ....
Я друг (подруга) (господина/госпожи) ....
ya drook (pa-DROO-ga) (ga-spa-DEE-na/ga-spa-ZHEE) ....

Keeping in mind that many Russian negotiators do not speak English,
foreign travelers will find it helpful to translate both their personal
names and their company names into a simple Russian equivalent.
Not only will the Russians appreciate the gesture, but they will be
more likely to remember the name.

My name is ....
Меня зовут ....
m'yen-YA za-VOOT ....

My company name is ....
Моя компания называется ....
ma-YA kahm-PA-nee-ya na-zee-VA-yit-sa ....

We are located in New York.
Мы расположены в Нью-Йорке.
mee rahs-pa-LO-zheh-nee v' new YORK-yeh.

London
Лондон

Washington
Вашингтои

Sydney
Сидней

Toronto
Торонто

Detroit
Детройт

Birmingham
Бирмингам

Los Angeles
Лос-Анджелес

Paris
Париж

Berlin
Берлин

Tokyo
Токио

MAKING AN APPOINTMENT

In almost all cases, the Russian agency will arrange the time and place for the meeting. It's essential to be on time for any meeting that's been arranged, since meeting space is in short supply, and another meeting may have been booked for the following hour.

Where are we meeting?
Где мы встретимся?
gd'yeh mee FSTR'YEH-teem-sa?

Is that your office?
Это ваш оффис?
EH-ta vahsh office?

Where is it located?
Где он расположен?
gd' YEH ohn rahs-pah-LOH-zhehn?

Can you give my driver directions?
Вы можете объяснить путь моему шоферу?
vee MO-zhe-t' yeh ahb-yahs-NIT poot may-yeh-MOO sha-F' YO-roo?

Please write down the address for me.
Пожалуйста, напишите адрес для меня.
pa-ZHAHL-sta, na-pee-SHEET-y' eh AHD-r' yehs dl' ya m' yehn-YA.

What day are we meeting?
В какой день мы встречаемся?
f ka-KOY dy' ehn mee fstry' eh-CHA-yehm-s' ya?

What time are we meeting?
В котором часу мы встречаемся?
f ka-TOH-rahm cha-SOO mee fstry' eh-CHA-yehm-s' ya?

How long will the meeting last?
Как долго продлится встреча?
kahk DOHL-ga prahd-LEET-sa VSTR' YEH-cha?

I'm looking forward to seeing you!
Я буду рад (рада) увидеть вас.
ya BOO-doo rahd (RA-da) oo-VEE-d' yet vahs.

I'll see you at the meeting.
Я увижу вас на встрече.
ya oo-VEE-zhoo vahs na FSTRY' EH-ch-yeh.

CONFIRMING AN APPOINTMENT

Although Western negotiators find this frustrating, the meeting will probably be confirmed only at the last minute. First-time visitors will receive lower priority than "old friends," so a new traveler should make a point of being available for the entire day, to maximize the chances of actually being seen. The foreign company's chamber of commerce or the commercial department of the appropriate embassy might also prove helpful in making sure that meetings happen within a reasonable length of time.

Are we still meeting today?
Мы еще встретимся сегодня?
mee yesh-CHO FSTR'YEH-teem-sa see-VOHD-n'ya?

Is our meeting at ...... o'clock?
Наша встреча в ...... часов?
NA-sha FSTRY'EH-cha f'...... cha-SOHF?

I am free all day.
Я свободен (свободна) целый день.
ya sva-BO-d'yehn (sva-BO-dna) TSEH-lee d'yehn.

I'd very much like to meet with you today.
Я очень хотел (хотела) бы встретиться с вами сегодня.
ya OH-chin kha-T'YEL (kha-T'YE-la) bee FSTR'YEH-ti-tsa s VA-mee see-VOHD-n'ya.

Can you meet with me today?
Вы можете встретиться со мной сегодня?
vee MO-zhee-t'yeh FSTRY'EH-teet-sa sa mnoy see-VOHD-n'ya?

BUSINESS TITLES

The Russians will try to determine the rank of foreign negotiators and select their own negotiators accordingly. Thus, it's important to stick to middle-level negotiators early in the process, since Russian middle management is far easier to deal with than the higher-ups. Likewise, foreign senior management should not appear to be intervening in negotiations on a daily basis, since that will undermine the Russians' confidence in the rest of the team. However, top management should be introduced to the Russians early on so that they will believe that the foreign enterprise is truly committed to the project. In the same vein, senior company officials should show up at social occasions, formal signings, and any other "official" events, to confirm the importance of the proceedings.

What is your rank?
Какая ваша позиция?
ka-KA-ya VA-sha pa-ZEE-tsee-ya?

Who is your superior?
Кто ваш начальник?
KTO vahsh na-CHAHL-neek?

I am president.
Я президент.
ya pry' eh-zee-DY' EHNT.

I am vice president.
Я вице-президент.
ya VEE-tseh-pry' eh-zee-DY' EHNT.

I am a manager.
Я менеджер.
ya M' YEH-n' yed-zhehr.

He/she is an engineer.
Он/Она инженер.
ohn/ah-NA een-zheh-N' YEHR.

He/she is a lawyer.
Он/Она адвокат.
ohn/ah-NA ahd-va-KAHT.

This is my superior, Mr./Ms. ....
Это мой начальник, господин/госпожа ....
EH-TA moy na-CHAHL-neek, gahs-pa-DEEN/gahs-pa-ZHA ....

My superior will be at the signing tomorrow.
Мой начальник будет завтра на подписании документов.
moy na-CHAHL-neek BOOD-yeht ZAHF-tra na
paht-pee-SA-nee-yee da-koo-M' YEHN-tahf.

SUBMITTING A PROPOSAL

Most of those who have dealt with Russian enterprises recommend submitting proposals to an enterprise, government agency, or other entity before the meeting is set up. Although releasing information in advance does give the Russian side a certain advantage, it may also reassure them that the foreign team is being straightforward and comprehensive in its presentation of material.

Have you seen our proposal?

Вы видели наше предложение?

vee VEED-yeh-lee NA-sheh preh-dla-ZHEH-nee-yeh?

We sent you a proposal last month.

Мы послали вам предложение в прошлом месяце.

mee pahs-LA-lee vahm preh-dla-ZHEH-nee-yeh f' PROHSH-lahm M'YEH-s'ya-tseh.

Here is our latest proposal.

Вот наше самое последнее предложение.

voht NA-sheh SA-ma-yeh pahs-L'YEHD-nee-yeh preh-dla-ZHEH-nee-yeh.

What did you think of our proposal?

Что вы думали о нашем предложении?

SHTO vee DOO-ma-lee ah NA-shehm preh-dla-ZHEH-nee-ee?

Do you wish to see a written proposal?

Вы хотите видеть письменное предложение?

vee ka-TEET-yeh VEED-yeht PEES-m'y eh-na-yeh preh-dla-ZHEH-nee-yeh?

What other information do you need?

Какая информация еще вам нужна?

ka-KA-ya een-fahr-MA-tsee-ya yish-CHO vahm noozh-NA?

Do you have any questions?

У вас есть вопросы?

oo vahs yehst vahp-RO-see?

(Mr./Ms.) ………… can answer that question.
(Господин/госпожа) ………… **может ответить на этот вопрос.**
(ga-spa-DEEN/ga-spa-ZHA) ………… MO-zheht
aht-V'YEH-teet na EH-taht vahp-ROHS.

(Mr./Ms.) ………… will call you about that.
(Господин/госпожа) ………… **позвонит вам об этом.**
(ga-spa-DEEN/ga-spa-ZHA) ………… pahz-va-NEET vahm
ahb EH-tahm.

(Mr./Ms.) ………… will send you that information.
(Господин/госпожа) ………… **пошлет вам эту информацию.**
(ga-spa-DEEN/ga-spa-ZHA) ………… pahsh-L'YOHT vahm
EH-too een-fohr-MA-tsee-y'oo.

I don't know, but I'll find out.
Я не знаю, но я узнаю.
YA n'yeh ZNA-yoo, no ya oo-ZNA-yoo.

I'll ask our engineering department.
Я спрошу наше инженерное отделение.
ya spra-SHOO NA-sheh een-zhee-NY'EHR-na-yeh aht-d'yel –
YEH-nee-yeh.

I'll ask my superior.
Я спрошу своего начальника.
ya spra-SHOO sva-yeh-VO na-CHAHL-nee-ka.

I'll ask our company president.
Я спрошу президента нашей компании.
ya spra-SHOO pry'eh-zee-D'YEHN-ta NA-shey kahm-PA-nee-ee.

PREPARING A CONTRACT

In a similar vein, foreign companies may find it helpful to prepare
their own contract in both Russian and the home country's language.
This preparation is particularly important when dealing with cooperatives and enterprises that were set up outside the Ministry for Foreign
Economic Relations, as these groups may not yet have either their
own contracts or any way to produce one. At some point, this contract

should be shared with the Russian side, in order to indicate the foreign company's intentions and way of doing business.

Here is a sample contract from our company.
Вот образец контракта от нашей компании.
voht ahb-ra-ZY'EHTS kahn-TRAHK-ta aht NA-shey kahm-PA-nee-ee.

This contract will help us to work together.
Этот контракт поможет нам работать вместе.
EH-taht kahn-TRAHKT pa-MO-zheht nahm ra-BO-taht VM'YEH-styeh.

This contract is open to negotiation.
Этот контракт открыт для переговоров.
EH-taht kahn-TRAHKT aht-KREET dl'ya pyeh-ryeh-ga-VO-rahf.

INTERPRETERS

Foreign travelers should not assume that all or even most of the negotiators on the Russian team will speak English. When the meeting is first arranged, both sides should agree on who will provide the interpreter.

Will you provide an interpreter?
Вы предоставите переводчика?
vee pr'yeh-da-STA-vee-t'yeh pyeh-ryeh-VOHD-chee-ka?

Do you want us to bring the interpreter?
Вы хотите, чтобы мы привезли переводчика?
vee kha-TEET-yeh, SHTO-bee mee pree-v'yehz-LEE pyeh-ryeh-VOHD-chee-ka?

Our colleague (Mr./Ms.) .... speaks Russian.
Наш (Наша) коллега (господин/госпожа) .... говорит по-русски.
nahsh (NA-sha) kahl-L'YEH-ga (ga-spa-DEEN/ ga-spa-ZHA) .... ga-va-REET pa-ROOS-kee.

I'm sorry that we don't speak Russian.
Извините, что мы не говорим по-русски.
eez-vee-NEE-t'yeh, shto mee n'yeh ga-va-REEM pa-ROOS-kee.

Thank you for providing the interpreter.
Спасибо за предоставление переводчика.
spa-SEE-ba za pr'yeh-da-sta-V'LYEHN-ee-yeh
pyeh-ryeh-VOHD-chee-ka.

TOWARD AN AGREEMENT

Coming to agreement about a contract is likely to take more than one meeting – possibly even more than one visit. The Russians are polite and efficient negotiators, but they must negotiate through a network of bureaucratic and technical personnel in the course of reaching a decision. They may not acknowledge the considerable expenditure of time, money, and personnel represented by the foreign company's simple presence in Russia. They are also operating within a climate of shortages – including, as we have seen, shortages of meeting space. For all these reasons, foreign business people are advised to be both firm and patient.

I have to return home soon.
Мне вскоре надо будет вернуться домой.
mn'yeh FSKO-r'yeh NA-da BOO-d'yet veer-NOO-ts'ya
da-MOY.

I must go home tomorrow.
Я должен (должна) завтра ехать домой.
ya DOHL-zhehn (dahl-ZHNA) ZAHF-tra YEH-khat da-MOY.

I must go home next week.
Я должен (должна) ехать домой на будущей неделе.
ya DOHL-zhehn (dahl-ZHNA) YEH-khaht da-MOY na
BOO-doosh-ch'yey n'yeh-D'YEH-l'yeh.

When can you decide?
Когда вы сможете принять решение?
kahk-DA vee SMO-zheh-t'yeh pree-N'YAHT ree-SHEH-nee-yeh?

We can't wait that long.
Мы не можем так долго ждать.
mee n'yeh MO-zhim tahk DOHL-ga zhdat.

We need an answer soon.
Нам нужен ответ скоро.
nahm NOO-zhehn aht-v'YET SKO-ra.

When can we meet again?
Когда мы можем встречатся снова?
kahg-DA mee MO-zhim fstry' eh-CHAHT-sa SNO-va?

CONDUCTING A
BUSINESS MEETING

7

THE MEETING PLACE

As we have seen, the meeting is likely to be in a room booked by the Russian negotiator, probably a special conference room set apart from the usual open-plan office area. If a foreign company is meeting with the head of an institute or the general director of a foreign trade organization, however, the group may convene in that official's private office.

Is this your office?
Это ваш оффис?
Eh-ta vahsh office?

What a beautiful office!
Какой красивый оффис!
ka-KOY kra-SEE-vee office.

What building is this?
Какое это здание?
ka-KO-y'eh EH-ta ZDA-nee-y'eh?

INTRODUCTIONS

Every series of negotiations should begin with general introductions and hand-shaking all around. Almost invariably, a foreign business visitor will meet with at least two Russian negotiators at a time. That way, each can corroborate the other's version of events to avoid misunderstandings in the future.

Please introduce me to your colleagues.
Пожалуйста, представьте меня вашим коллегам.
pa-ZHAHL-sta, pry'eht-STAHF-t'yeh my'eh-N'YA VA-sheem ka-L'YEH-gahm.

I am happy to meet you both.
Рад (Рада) познакомиться с вами.
raht (RA-da) paz-na-KO-meet-s'ya ss VA-mee.

BUSINESS CARDS

Exchanging business cards printed in both languages is an essential part of the introductory ritual, and foreign visitors should make sure to carry enough cards to supply all members of the Russian team. If Russians apologize for not having enough of their cards – usually because of delays at the printer – foreign negotiators should ask them to write down their names and other key data on a piece of paper. This request won't offend the Russians, who understand the importance of exchanging these data in order to maintain contact and keep clear records of who attended a meeting.

Welcome!
Добро пожаловать!
dahb-RO pa-ZHA-la-vaht!

We are happy to meet you.
Мы радуемся познакомиться с вами.
mee RA-doo-yim-sa pa-zna-KO-mit-sa z'VA-mi.

Thank you for coming to this meeting.
Спасибо, что вы пришли на эту встречу.
spa-SEE-ba, shto vee preesh-LEE na EH-too FSTR'YEH-choo.

We are glad to see you here!
Мы рады видеть вас здесь!
mee RA-dee VEE-d'yet vahs zd'yes!

My name is .... from the .... company.
Меня зовут .... и я из компании ....
m'ye-N'YA za-VOOT .... ee ya eez
kahm-PA-nee-yee ....

Here is my card.
Вот моя визитная карточка.
voht ma-YA vee-ZEET-na-ya KA-tahch-ka.

May I have your card?
Могу я взять вашу визитную карточку?
ma-GOO ya vz'yaht VA-shoo vee-ZEET-noo-yoo
KAR-tahch-koo?

COMPANY PROFILES

In addition to business cards, it's a good idea for foreign visitors to have a brief profile of their company, translated into Russian. This profile can be presented to the other side after the initial exchange of business cards.

Here is some information about our company.
Вот информация о нашей компании.
voht een-fohr-MA-tsee-ya ah NA-shey kahm-PA-nee-ee.

This includes our records for the past year.
Это включает наши отчеты за последний год.
EH-ta fkl' yoo-CHA-yit NA-shee aht-CH'YO-tee za pahs-L'YEHD-nee goht.

FORMS OF ADDRESS

Courtesy of address is important to Russian negotiators. They will turn to first names much more slowly than is customary in English-speaking countries, and will expect their foreign guests to respect this custom. Russians may refer to colleagues by their first names, but foreign visitors should defer this intimacy for at least the first few meetings.

It's also acceptable to call a Russian by two names – either first name plus family name (e.g., Mikhail Gorbachev) or first name plus patronymic (the name that means "son of" or "daughter of," e.g., Mikhail Sergeyevich [son of Sergey] or Marya Sergeyevna [daughter of Sergey]). The Russian language includes several nicknames, which, once again, foreigners should avoid. (For example, "Mikhail" may be abbreviated as "Misha" or "Mishka"; "Alexandr" may become "Sasha" etc.) The safest policy is to use the name written on the Russian's business card. If necessary, the Russian businessperson may be asked what the initials on his or her card stand for.

Russians do appreciate the extra "Russian-ness" of visitors using a patronymic, which is slightly less formal than saying "Mr." or "Ms." but still less intimate than the first name alone.

Male and female officials in Russia may both be addressed by title.

CONDUCTING A MEETING

Director
Директор
dee-R'YEHK-tohr

Manager
Менеджер
M'YEH-n'yehd-zhehr

Chief engineer
Главный инженер
GLAHV-nee een-zhee-N'YEHR

What do these initials stand for?
Эти инициалы сокращение чего?
EH-tee ee-nee-tsee-AH-lee sa-krahsh-CH'YEH-nee-yeh ch'yi-VO?

What is your full name?
Как ваше полное имя?
kahk VA-sheh POHL-na-yeh EE-m'ya?

SMALL TALK

Meetings usually begin with small talk, despite the limited time that may be available. Appropriate topics include the weather, holidays, non-controversial current events, and remarks or anecdotes about one's own country. Foreign negotiators should expect to match Russian proverbs and national anecdotes with their own.

What a lovely day!
Какой приятный день!
ka-KOY pree-YAHT-nee d'yen!

Is it likely to snow?
Вероятно, что будет снег?
v'yi-ra-YAHT-na, shto BOO-dyeht sn'yekh?

Did you have a pleasant weekend?
Вы проводили конец недели приятно?
vee pra-va-DEE-lee ka-N'YETS n'yeh-D'YEH-lee pree-YAHT-na?

I'm enjoying my stay in your city very much.
Мне нравится быть в вашем городе.
mn' yeh NRA-veet-sa beet v VA-shehm GO-ra-d' yeh.

The Russians prefer to conduct negotiations in an atmosphere of comfort and courtesy. To this end, they will provide mineral water and Pepsi-Cola, tea, coffee, cookies, and cakes at the conference table.

What delicious coffee!
Какой вкусный кофе!
ka-KOY FKOOS-nee KO-f' yeh!

May I have some more mineral water?
Можно мне еще минеральной воды?
mohzh-na mn' yeh yish-CHO mee-neh-RAHL-noy va-DEE?

Please pass the Pepsi-Cola.
Передайте, пожалуйста Пепсн-Колу.
p' yee-ree-DAY-t' yeh, pa-ZHAHL-sta, PEP-see-KO-loo.

Thank you for the cake.
Спасибо за торт.
spa-SEE-ba za tort.

I'd like some cookies, please.
Я хотел (хотела) бы немного печенья, пожалуйста.
*ya kha-T' YEHL (kha-T' YEH-la) bee
neh-MNO-ga peh-CH' YEH-nee-ya, pa-ZHAHL-sta.*

THE NEGOTIATIONS

The usual hour for negotiations to begin is 9 a.m., with a long lunch break beginning at 1 p.m. Although negotiations may resume after lunch – which may last until 3 p.m. or 4 p.m. – they are unlikely to last very long. Negotiations are almost never scheduled during evenings and weekends – a time during which foreigners often profit by studying the documents produced at the meeting of the day.

Is it time for lunch?
Уже время обеда?
oo-ZHEH VR'YEH-m'ya ah-B'YEH-da?

When will we break for lunch?
Когда будет перерыв на обед?
kahk-DA BOO-d'yit p'yeh-R'YEH-REEV na ah-B'YEHT?

Can we continue this discussion after lunch?
Мы можем продолжить эту дискуссию после обеда?
*mee MO-zhehm pra-DOHL-zheet EH-too dees-KOO-see-yoo
POHS-l'yeh ahb-YEH-da?*

When do we meet tomorrow?
Когда мы встретимся завтра?
kahg-DA mee FSTR'YEH-teem-sa ZAHF-tra?

I'm looking forward to talking more soon!
Я ожидаю, с удовольствием что мы еще поговорим вскоре.
*ya ah-zhee-DA-yoo s oo-da-VOHL-stvee-yem, shto mee
yeh-SHCHO pa-ga-va-REEM FSKOR-yeh.*

Russian negotiators will respond best to firm politeness. But foreign negotiators who appear inflexible may provoke an end to the negotiations; therefore, it is important to avoid saying "no" even to apparently outrageous demands. Instead, negotiators should find a way to appear willing to at least consider every proposal.

Should we take a short break?
Нужен ли нам короткий перерыв?
NOO-zhehn lee nahm ka-ROHT-kee p'yeh-r'yeh-REEF?

I'm sure we can agree.
Я уверен(а), что мы можем договориться.
ya oo-V'YEH-r'yehn(a), shto mee MO-zhehm da-ga-va-REE-ts'ya.

I think we need to talk further.
Я думаю, что нам надо обсуждать это дальше.
ya DOO-ma-oo, shto nahm NA-do ahp-soo-ZHDAT EH-ta DAHL-sheh.

Where do you disagree?
С чем вы не согласны?
ss chehm vee n'yeh sa-GLA-snee?

Which points don't you accept?
Каких пунктов вы не принимаете?
ka-KEEKH POONK-tahf vee n'yeh pree-nee-MA-yeh-t'yeh?

Can you explain it once more?
Вы можете объяснить снова?
vee MO-zheh-t'yeh ahb-yahs-NEET SNOH-va?

I want to be sure I understand.
Я хочу быть уверен(а) в том, что правильно понял (поняла).
ya kha-CHOO beet oo-VY'EHR-yehn(a) f tohm, shtoh
PRA-veel-nah PO-n'yahl (pa-n'yah-LA).

This meeting will produce good results for both companies.
Эта встреча принесет хорошие результаты для обеих компаний.
EH-ta FSTRY'EH-cha pree-nee-SY'OHT kha-RO-shee-y'eh
ry'eh-zool-TA-tee dly'a ah-BEH-eekh kahm-PA-nee.

I have a problem with Clause Number ....
У меня проблема с пунктом номер ....
oo m'ye-N'YA prahb-L'YEH-ma ss'POONK-tahm
NO-m'yehr ....

I don't understand this point.
Я не понимаю этого пуикта.
ya n'yeh pa-nee-MA-yoo EH-ta-va POONK-ta.

Russian negotiators will expect their foreign counterparts to talk in very specific terms. They will ask for a great deal of detailed information, especially since they usually can't travel to the foreign country to view the technology for themselves. Visitors who can't readily answer detailed technical questions will find themselves the objects of either suspicion or lack of respect.

What else would you like to know?
Что еще вы хотите знать?
shto yeh-SHCHO vee kha-TEET-yeh znaht?

Could you please repeat your question?
Вы можете повторить свой вопрос, пожалуйста?
vee MO-zheh-t' yeh pahf-ta-REET svoy va-PROHS, pa-ZHAHL-sta?

Perhaps I haven't been clear.
Возможно, я был (была) не ясен (ясна).
vahz-MOHZH-na, ya beel (bee-LA) n' yeh YA-s' yehn (yis-NA).

I can get that information for you in writing.
Я могу достать эту информацию для вас в письменном виде.
ya ma-GOO dahs-TAHT EH-too een-for-MA-tsee-yoo dl' ya vahs f PEES-m' yeh-nohm VEED-yeh.

I will call our home office.
Я позвоню нашему оффису у нас в родине.
ya pahz-va-N' YOO NA-shee-moo OH-fee-soo oo nahs v RO-dee-n' yeh.

I will give you that information tomorrow.
Я вам дам эту инфомацию завтра.
ya vahm dahm EH-too een-for-MA-tsee-yoo ZAHF-tra.

Mr./Mrs. ....
has that information.
Эта информация у господина/госпожи ....
EH-ta een-for-MA-tsee-ya oo ga-spa-DEE-na/ ga-spa-ZHEE ....

He/She will be at our meeting tomorrow.
Он/Она будет на нашей завтрашней встрече.
ohn/ah-NA BOO-d' yeht na NA-shey ZAHF-trahsh-n' yey FSTR' YEH-ch' e.

GIFTS

The Russians are very attached to gift-giving as a way to cement friendships and business relationships. Russian gifts to foreign visitors may be in the nature of souvenirs, such as wooden handicrafts, records, or Russian dolls; they may also present visitors with high-quality "coffee-table" books on Russian art. Between November and the end of February, many Russian businesses exchange calendars with their business partners.

Thank you very much!
Большое спасибо!
bahl-SHO-yeh spa-SEE-ba!

What a beautiful present!
Какой красивый подарок!
ka-KOY kra-SEE-vee pa-DA-rahk!

My colleagues in the United States will admire this.
Мои коллеги в США этим восхитятся.
ma-YEE kah-L'YEH-gee f SS'SHA EH-teem vahs-kheet-YAHT-sa.

My family will enjoy this.
Моей семье это понравится.
ma-yeh-ee s'yeh-M'YEH EH-ta pahn-RA-veet-sa.

I will always remember this.
Я всегда буду это помнить.
ya fsy'ehg-DA BOO-doo EH-ta POHM-neet.

I appreciate this token of your friendship.
Я ценю этот знак вашей дружбы.
ya tseh-N'YOO EH-taht znahk VA-shey DROOZH-bee.

I can really use this calendar!
Я действительно могу использовать этот календарь!
ya dey-STVEE-t'yehl-na MA-goo ees-POHL-za-vaht EH-taht ka-l'yehn-DAR.

GETTING AROUND WITHIN A CITY

8

In some cases, business travelers may be provided a car and driver by their host organization. In other cases, a traveler may wish to go by taxi. (For information and phrases relating to taxis, see "At the Hotel.") However, other means of transportation are available in most Russian cities, particularly Moscow and St. Petersburg.

CAR RENTAL

In Moscow, most hotels catering to foreign business travelers may rent cars with or without drivers. The Intourist Service Bureau also rents cars with or without drivers. In any case, all arrangements at the hotels are made through Intourist. Cars must be paid for in hard currency. In St. Petersburg, it's a good idea to rent a chauffeur-driven car in advance, since it's very difficult to get cabs there and since many of the best hotels are outside the city center. A chauffeur-driven car can be rented in advance through Intourist or at hotels, which tend to want to rent cars for a half day at a time.

I'd like to rent a car with a driver, please.
Я хочу взять на прокат машину с шофером, пожалуйста.
Ya kha-CHOO vz'yaht na pra-KAHT ma-SHEE-noo ss'sha-F'YO-rahm, pa-ZHA-lsta.

I've already reserved a car and driver.
Я уже забронировал (забронировала) машину н шофера.
ya oo-ZHEH za-bra-NEE-ra-vahl (za bra-NEE-ra-va-la) ma-SHEE-noo ee sha-F'YO-ra.

I made the arrangements through Intourist.
Я организовал(а) через "Интурист".
ya ahr-ga-nee-za-VAHL(a) CHEH-r'yehz "een-too-RIST".

How soon will a car and driver be available?
Когда я смогу использовать машину и шофера?
kahg-DA ya sma-GOO ees-POHL-za-vaht ma-SHEE-noo ee sha-F'YO-ra?

Where else can I rent a car with a driver?
Где еще я могу взять на прокат машину с шофером?
gd'yeh yeesh-CHO ya ma-GOO vz'yaht na pra-KAHT ma-SHEE-noo s sha-F'YOH-rahm?

How much does it cost to rent a car with driver?
Сколько стоит взять на прокат машину с шофером?
*SKOHL-ka STO-eet vz'yaht na pra-KAHT ma-SHEE-noo
ss'sha-F'YO-rahm?*

I would like to rent by the day.
Я хочу брать на прокат по дню.
ya kha-CHOO braht na pra-KAHT pa dn'yoo.

I would like to rent by the half-day.
Я хочу брать на прокат по половине дня.
ya kha-CHOO braht na pra-kaht pa pa-la-VEE-n'yeh dn'ya.

I would like to rent by the hour.
Я хочу брать на прокат по часу.
ya kha-CHOO braht na pra-KAHT pa CHA-soo.

Cars without drivers are not recommended to first-time visitors, who may have difficulty negotiating Russian cities' complicated maze of streets. Potholes, icy streets, poor lighting, and Cyrillic directional signs are further hazards for new drivers.

Visitors who do want to drive in Russia will need an international driver's license in addition to their home country's license. Traffic keeps to the right in Russia. In Moscow, parking is allowed virtually everywhere except Red Square and the Kremlin; yellow lines, and tram and bus stops are also off limits. The speed limit is 60 kilometers or 37 miles per hour.

I'd like to rent a car, please.
Я хочу взять на прокат машину, пожалуйста.
ya kha-CHOO vz'yaht na pra-KAHT ma-SHEE-noo, pa-ZHAHL-sta.

I'll only be using it within the city.
Я буду использовать ее только в городе.
ya BOO-doo ees-POHL-za-vaht yeh-YO TOHL-ka f'GO-ra-d'yeh.

Do you have a street map?
У вас есть план улиц?
oo vahs yehst plahn OO-leets?

How do I get to ....?
Как доехать до ....?
kahk da-YEH-khaht da ....?

Here is my home driver's license and here is my international license.
Вот мои шоферские права и вот мои международные права.
*voht ma-EE sha-F'YOHR-skee-yeh pra-VA ee voht ma-EE
meezh-doo-na-ROHD-nee-yeh pra-VA.*

Traffic Police

Most drivers remove their windshield wipers when they leave their cars, as petty thievery is on the increase since the opening up of the free market. Traffic police strictly enforce the law; they can be recognized by their black-and-white striped clubs. Notably, though, police in Russia are not allowed to carry guns.

I'm sorry; I am a foreigner.
Извините, я иностранец/иностранка.
eez-vee-NEE-tyeh, ya ee-na-STRAHN-etz (-ka).

Excuse me, I won't do it again.
Извините, я этого больше не сделаю.
eez-vee-NEE-t'yeh, ya EH-ta-va BOHL-sheh n'yeh SD'YEH-la-yoo.

TAXIS

If a traveler is going by taxi, he or she should either be able to clearly pronounce the destination in Russian or should have the address written in Cyrillic. (The hotel service bureau may be helpful in this regard.) In Moscow and St. Petersburg, you will find taxis waiting outside most large hotels. If the service desk calls you a taxi, you may have to wait up to an hour before it arrives.

Can you call a taxi for me, please?
Вы можете вызвать для меня такси?
vee MO-zhee-t'yeh VEEZ-vaht dl'ya meh-N'YA tahk-SEE?

How long will it take?
Как долго это продлится?
kahk DOHL-ga EH-ta pra-DLEE-tsa?

113

Can you write the address down for me?
Вы можете написать адрес для меня?
vee MO-zheh-t' yeh na-pee-SAHT AHD-rehs dl' ya meh-N'YA?

Here is where I want to go.
Вот куда я хочу поехать.
voht koo-DA ya kha-CHOO pa-YEN-khaht.

Do you have change?
У вас мелочь?
oo vahs M'YEH-lahch?

What is the fare?
Какая цена?
ka-KA-ya tseh-NA?

Foreigners are often expected to bargain with hard currency or Western cigarettes. Since this is technically illegal, business travelers should use their own judgment in this regard.

Here is a pack of Western cigarettes.
Вот пачка западных сигарет.
voht PAHCH-ka ZA-pahd-neekh see-ga-R'YEHT.

I can only pay in roubles.
Я могу платить только в рублях.
ya ma-GOO pla-TEET TOHL-ka v roob-L'YAHKH.

That fare is too high.
Эта цена слишком высокая.
EH-ta tseh-NA SLEESH-kahm vee-SO-ka-ya.

THE METRO

Public transport in Russia is efficient and relatively easy for the foreign traveler to understand once he or she can sound out the Cyrillic alphabet.

In Moscow, the famous metro system is the most extensive in the world, with few points even in the suburbs that are further than half an hour from the city center. It's generally faster to take the train than to travel by taxi, if one is near a metro station. Most places in Moscow are within a fifteen-minute walk of a metro station, which is marked by a large M on a white background, lit up at night.

Almost all riders ride in silence in the Moscow metro, even during the rush hour. Metro stations are decorated with mosaics, marble columns, chandeliers, and other tributes to former Soviet workers and peasants. Each station has change machines and coin-driven turnstiles; every station is equipped with maps; every station is announced on the train.

St. Petersburg's metro system is also cheap, efficient, and well-decorated. It too is marked with large white M signs – and every hotel has a nearby station.

Where is the nearest metro station?
Где самая близкая метростанция?
gd'yeh SA-ma-ya BLEES-ka-ya mee-tra-STAHN-tsee-ya?

I want to go to ....; which stop is that?
Я хочу доехать до ....; какая это остановка?
ya kha-CHOO da-YEH-khaht da ....; ka-KA-ya EH-ta ahs-ta-NOHF-ka?

How many stops to ....?
Сколько остановок до ....?
SKOHL-ka ahs-ta-NO-vahk da ....?

Where is the map?
Где городской план?
gd'yeh ga-raht-SKOY plahn?

Where can I get change?
Где я могу получить мелочь?
gd'yeh ya ma-GOO pa-loo-CHEET M'YEH-lach?

ON FOOT

By the way, in good weather, it's a pleasure to walk through most Russian cities, including Moscow and St. Petersburg. Sidewalks are wide and well-maintained. Although foreigners may find themselves besieged by black-marketeers or petty entrepreneurs, they will also find Russian citizens extremely helpful and hospitable. Most Russians do not speak English, but will nonetheless help a stranger find his or her way if possible.

I want to go to............
Я хочу дойти до ....
ya kha-CHOO da-ee-TEE da ....

Where is that on the map?
Где это на плане?
gd' yeh EH-ta na PLA-n' yeh?

Thank you for your help!
Спасибо за вашу помощь!
spa-SEE-ba za VA-shoo PO-mashch!

Your city is very beautiful!
Ваш город очень красивый!
vahsh GO-raht OH-chehn kra-SEE-vee!

TRAVEL BETWEEN CITIES

9

BY AIR

Most business travelers will fly from city to city within Russia, although Aeroflot, the national – and only – Russian airline, is notorious for poor service. Western experts have also estimated that Aeroflot has one of the worst safety records in the world. Reportedly, service is improving, however.

To the airport, please.
В аэропорт, пожалуйста.
v' ah-eh-ra-POHRT, pa-ZHA-lsta.

How long does it take to go to the airport?
Как долго до аэропорта?
kahk DOHL-ga doh ah-eh-ro-POHR-ta?

How long does the flight to .... take?
Как долго лететь до ....?
kahk DOHL-ga l' yeh-T'YEHT da ....?

I want a ticket to ....
Я хочу билет в ....
ya kha-CHOO bee-L'YEHT v' ....

Making and Changing Reservations

If at all possible, reservations for long-distance travel should be made in advance, so that a specialist travel agent can assure the foreign traveler of confirmation. Within Russia, Intourist hotel service desks can arrange a trip, as well as reserve a car to meet the foreign traveler at the airport or railway station.

I've already made these reservations.
Я уже забронировал(а)
ya oo-ZHEH za-bra-NEE-ro-VAHL(a).

I'd like to confirm my reservation.
Я хочу подтвердить свою броню.
ya kha-CHOO paht-vehr-DEET sva-YOO BRO-n' yoo.

Where can I make reservations?

Где я могу забронировать?

gd'yeh ya ma-GOO za-bra-NEE-ra-vaht?

Can you arrange for a driver to meet me?

Вы можете организовать, чтобы шофер встретил меня?

vee MO-zhee-t'yeh ahr-ga-nee-zo-VAHT, SHTO-bee sha-F'YOHR fstr'yeh-TEEL meh-N'YA?

Changing reservations in Russia is extremely difficult. Any changes made at 24 hours notice will be penalized by 10%; a change within 3 hours costs 25% of the fare; a change less than 3 hours before flight time will not be refunded. Flights are usually booked solid, and a traveler's preference will play little part in the flight that he or she is reassigned.

I'd like to change my reservation.

Я хочу изменить свою броню.

ya kha-CHOO eez-m'yeh-NEET sva-YOO BRO-n'yoo.

I'd like to cancel my reservation.

Я хочу отменить свою броню.

ya kha-CHOO aht-meh-NEET sva-YOO BRO-n'yoo.

How much will it cost to cancel?

Сколько эта отмена будет стоить?

SKOHL-ka EH-ta aht-M'YEH-na BOO-d'yeht STO-eet?

Travel Times

In the West, travel times are given according to the time zone in which they are located. Thus, a New York–California flight will give the departure time in New York time and the arrival time in California time. In Russia, all timetables are given in Moscow time. Thus, travelers should check to find out what the hour will be in their actual destination.

When do I arrive?

Когда я приезжаю?

kahg-DA ya pree-yehzh-ZHA-yoo?

Is that Moscow time or local time?
Это московское или местное время?
EH-ta mahs-KOHF-ska-yeh EE-lee M'YEHST-na-yeh VREH-m'ya?

What time is that in local time?
Который это час по местному времени?
ka-TOH-ree EH-ta chahs pa M'YEHST-na-moo VREH-m'yeh-nee?

Travel Vouchers

Visitors whose flights are prearranged are usually given a single travel voucher, which should be turned into the hotel service bureau on arrival. The bureau will then issue a ticket for the next stage of the journey, along with a new voucher to be handed in at the next stop. Travelers are advised to check their vouchers and tickets carefully to ensure against error. They should be particularly careful that the correct fare has been deducted.

Here is my voucher.
Вот мой ваучер.
voht moy VOW-chehr.

When will my next ticket be ready?
Когда мой будущий билет будет готов?
kahg-DA moy BOO-doosh-chee bee-L'YEHT BOO-d'yet ga-TOHF?

I'm leaving tomorrow; I must have my ticket by then!
Я уезжаю завтра; мне нужен билет перед этим.
ya oo-yehzh-ZHA-yoo ZAHF-tra;
mn'yeh NOO-zhehn bee-L'YEHT P'YEH-reed EH-teem.

There is a mistake on this voucher.
Есть ошибка на этом ваучере.
yehst ah-SHEEP-ka na EH-tahm VOW-cheh-r'yeh.

This ticket has the wrong time.
На этом билете неправильное время.
na EH-tahm bee-L'YEH-t'yeh nee-PRA-veel-na-yeh VREH-m'ya.

You have deducted the wrong amount here.

Вы вычли неправильную сумму.

vee VEECH-lee nee-PRA-veel-noo-yoo SOO-moo.

At the Airport

Aeroflot's on-time record is very good in summer, but, in winter, bad weather may bring unforeseen and unpreventable delays. Thus, travelers may wish to travel by train for shorter distances in winter. Throughout Russia, foreign travelers have access to a special lounge, with somewhat better facilities than in the rest of the airport. Occasionally, canned drinks, cigarettes, and souvenirs are for sale; at the very least, foreigners will be able to find seating. At many airports, smoking is banned.

Where is the foreigners' lounge?

Где комната отдыха для иностранцев?

gd' yeh KOM-na-ta OHT-dee-kha dl' ya ee-na-STRAHN-tsehf?

Where is the toilet?

Где туалет?

gd' yeh twa-L'YEHT?

Can I buy something to eat?

Могу я купить что-нибудь поесть?

ma-GOO ya koo-PEET SHTO-nee-boot pa-YEHST?

Can I buy something to drink?

Могу я купить что-нибудь попить?

ma-GOO ya koo-PEET SHTO-nee-boot pa-PEET?

Is there an airport store?

В аэропорту есть магазин?

v' ah-eh-ro-pahr-TOO yehst ma-ga-ZEEN?

Where do I check in for this flight?

Где мне регистрироваться на этот полет?

gd' yeh mn' yeh reh-gees-TREE-ro-va-tsa na EH-taht pa-L'YOHT?

Has flight Number .... been delayed?
Полет номер .... задерживается?
pa-L'YOHT NO-m'yehr............ za-D'YEHR-zhee-va-y'eh tsa?

When will my flight leave?
Когда мой полет отбывает?
kahk-DA moy pa-L'YOT aht-bee-VA-yeht?

How long will we wait?
Как долго нам ждать?
kahk DOHL-ga nahm zhdaht?

When will you have more information?
Когда у вас будет больше информации?
kahg-DA oo vahs BOO-d'yeht BOHL-sheh een-fohr-MA-tsee-ee?

On the Plane

Usually, foreign travelers are allowed to board first and are seated at the front of the aircraft. Theoretically, this is the "first-class" section, although in fact the seats and service are identical throughout. Mineral water or fruit drink is available on short flights; a small snack is available on flights of four hours or more. There is no smoking on any Russian flight.

Excuse me, may I have something to drink?
Извините, могу я что-нибудь попить?
eez-vee-NEE-t'yeh, ma-GOO ya SHTO-nee-boot pa-PIT?

May I have something to eat?
Могу я что-нибудь поесть?
ma-GOO ya SHTO-nee-boot pa-YEHST?

When do we arrive?
Когда мы прилетаем?
kahg-DA mee pree-l'yeh-TA-yehm?

Couriers

Intourist couriers will meet foreign travelers at the airport for both arrival and departure, helping them negotiate baggage check-in and check-out and frequently enabling them to bypass lines. This airport–hotel transfer should be booked before you leave for Russia. Couriers generally speak English, but, like other Russians, appreciate the courtesy of a Russian phrase or two.

Where do I pick up my bags?
Где я получаю свой багаж?
gd' yeh ya pa-loo-CHA-yoo svoy ba-GAHZH?

Can you help me get to the .... Hotel?
Вы можете помочь мне доехать до гостиницы ....?
vee MO-zhee-t' yeh pa-MOHCH mn' yeh da-YEH-khaht da gahs-TEE-nee-tsee............?

I've arranged for a car to pick me up; where would it be?
Я организовал машину встретить меня; где она будет ждать?
ya ahr-ga-nee-za-VAHL ma-SHEE-noo fstr' yeh-TEET' meh-N'YA; gd' yeh ah-NA BOO-d' yeht zhdaht?

BY RAIL

As we have seen, shorter trips should be arranged by train, especially in winter. The journey from Moscow to St. Petersburg, for example, takes only eight hours by the average train (traveling at 70 kilometers or 43 miles per hour), and just over four hours by express. The trip from Moscow to Kiev takes about 10 hours. Travelers who are more interested in sightseeing than in saving time will find that the Russian rail system is extensive, punctual, and reliable. As with air schedules, train timetables are always given in Moscow time only.

To the railroad station, please.
К железнодорожной станции, пожалуйста.
k' zheh-l' yehz-na-da-ROHZH-noy STAHN-tsee-yee, pa-ZHAHL-sta.

I want a ticket to ....
Я хочу билет в ....
ya kha-CHOO bee-L'YEHT v............

How long is the trip to ....?
Как долго до ....?
kahk DOHL-ga da ....?

When does this train reach ....?
Когда этот поезд прибывает в ....?
kahg-DA EH-taht PO-yehst pree-bee-VA-yeht v' ....?

Is that Moscow time or local time?
Это московское или местное время?
EH-ta mahs-KOHF-ska-yeh EE-lee M'YEHST-na-yeh VREH-m'ya?

When does the train leave?
Когда поезд отбывает?
kahg-DA PO-yehst aht-bee-VA-yeht?

Is there an earlier train to ....?
Есть ли более ранний поезд в ....?
yehst lee BO-lee-yeh RA-nee PO-yehst v' ....?

Is there a later train to ....?
Есть ли более поздний поезд в ....?
yehst lee BO-lee-yeh POHZ-nee PO-yehst v' ....?

Can I still make reservations for the date of ....?
Могу ли я еще сделать брони на дату ....?
ma-GOO lee ya yeesh-CHO ZD'YEH-laht BRO-ni na DA-too............?

Making and Changing Reservations

Foreigners should make train reservations to guarantee their itineraries. It's best to make arrangements outside Russia, but hotel service desks and Intourist can help after arrival. Night sleepers are usually booked a week in advance, particularly between Moscow and St. Petersburg.

Cancellations up to six hours in advance are penalized by a small amount; later cancellations are not refundable. Rail service is about the same price as air service (which is low by international standards). Each ticket guarantees a particular seat.

I want to change my reservation on this train.

Я хочу изменить свою броню на этот поезд.

ya kha-CHOO eez-m'yeh-NEET sva-YOO BRO-n'yoo na EH-taht PO-yehst.

I want to cancel my reservation on this train.

Я хочу отменить свою броню на этот поезд.

ya kha-CHOO aht-m'yeh-NEET sva-YOO BRO-n'yoo na EH-taht PO-yehst.

I want a first-class ticket.

Я хочу билет первого класса.

ya kha-CHOO bee-L'YEHT PEHR-va-va KLA-sa.

I want a deluxe compartment.

Я хочу купе люкс.

ya kha-CHOO koo-PEH l'yooks.

I want an upper berth.

Я хочу верхнее место.

ya kha-CHOO VEHRKH-neeyeh M'YEHS-ta.

I want a lower berth.

Я хочу нижнее место.

ya kha-CHOO NEEZH-nee-yeh M'YEHS-ta.

On the Train

First-class or deluxe compartments are usually recommended for foreigners. These accommodations are clean and pleasant. There are either two or four berths in night sleepers, complete with clean bed linen and tea served by cabin attendants. Washrooms with hot water are located at the end of each corridor. There are no dining cars on trains traveling for less than eight hours, so passengers bring their own supplies on shorter journeys. Although railway stations are crowded, passengers can usually avoid the crush by boarding their trains without delay.

Where is seat number ....?

Где место номер ....?

gd'yeh M'YEHS-ta NO-m'yehr ....?

Where is the washroom?
Где туалет?
gd' yeh twa-L'YEHT?

Can I have some tea?
Могу я попить чаю?
ma-GOO ya pa-PEET CHA-yoo?

Is food sold on this train?
Продается еда на этом поезде?
pra-da-YO-tsya yeh-DA na EH-tahm PO-yehs-d' yeh?

Can I buy food at this station?
Могу я купить еду на этой станции?
ma-GOO ya koo-PEET yeh-DOO na EH-toy STAHN-tsee?

Can I buy something to drink at this station?
Могу я купить что-нибудь попить на этой станции?
*ma-GOO ya koo-PEET SHTO-nee-boot pa-PEET na
EH-toy STAHN-tsee-yee?*

What time is breakfast served?
Когда подается завтрак?
kahg-DA pa-da-YOHT-s' ya ZAHF-trahk?

What time is lunch served?
Когда подается обед?
kahg-DA pa-da-YOHT-s' ya ah-B'YEHT?

What time is dinner served?
Когда подается ужин?
kahg-DA pa-da-YOHT-sya OO-zheen?

EXCHANGING AND OBTAINING MONEY

10

The basic unit of Russian currency is known as the *rouble*. The rouble was once worth $1.35 at the official Soviet exchange rate – and about $.18 at the black-market rate. Although there were obvious financial advantages to foreigners exchanging on the black market, penalties were severe, including the possibility of deportation and future refusal of visas.

Today the official market rate for tourists is far more in line with the rouble's actual value on the world market, although the business exchange rate is still high. You will need to check what the official rate is before visiting Russia as it is changing constantly.

Roubles come in denominations of 1, 3, 5, 10, 25, 50, 100, 1000, 5,000, 10,000 and 50,000. The larger notes can be difficult to change, so for minor purchases, smaller notes are best.

The rouble is worth 100 kopeks. Kopeks come in coins worth 1, 2, 3, 5, 10, 15, 20, and 50 kopeks. Because of inflation, few items cost less than one rouble; 50 kopeks are rarely used.

EXCHANGING MONEY

Money can easily be changed at hotels or at the airport. Hotel exchange desks will accept actual foreign currency and traveler's checks as well as credit card cash advances.

Where can I exchange money?
Где я могу обменять деньги?
gd'yeh ya ma-GOO ahb-m'yeh-N'YAHT D'YEHN-gee?

Can you change this bill for me?
Вы можете обменять этот банкнот для меня?
vee MO-zhee-t'yeh ahb-m'ye-N'YAHT EH-taht bahn-KNOHT dl'ya m'yeh-N'ya.

I would prefer smaller bills, please.
Я хотел (хотела) бы меньшие банкноты, пожалуйста.
ya kha-T'YEHL (kha-T'YEH-la) bee M'YEHN-shee-yeh bahn-KNO-tee, pa-ZHAHL-sta.

I need some (small) change.
Мне нужна мелочь.
mn'yeh noozh-NA M'YEH-lahch.

MONEY

In order to exchange money, travelers must show their hotel identity card. Not only is a passport not necessary, it is frequently not accepted. In addition, travelers must produce their customs declaration form, to which certificates for each exchange of money must be attached. Without these records, a traveler will not be able to reconvert roubles to hard currency at the end of a trip – and black marketeers will not be able to profit from currency exchange. Thus a traveler buying on the black market is not only risking severe penalties, but also faces being saddled with many unconvertible roubles at trip's end.

Here is my hotel identity card.
Вот мое удостоверение личности из гостиницы.
voht ma-yo oo-da-sta-vee-R'YEH-nee-yeh LEECH-nahs-tee eez gahs-TEE-nee-tsee.

Here is my customs declaration form.
Вот моя таможенная декларация.
voht ma-YA ta-MO-zheh-na-ya dee-kla-RA-tsee-ya.

Please give me my certificate of exchange.
Дайте мне, пожалуйста, справку об обмене.
DAEE-t'yeh mn'yeh pa-ZHAHL-sta SPRA-fkoo ahb ahb-M'YEH-n'yeh.

Excuse me, you forgot to give me a receipt.
Извините, вы забыли дать мне квитанцию.
eez-vee-NEE-t'yeh, vee za-BEE-lee daht mn'yeh kvee-TAHN-tsee-yoo.

TRAVELER'S CHECKS

Major traveler's checks – American Express, Bank of America, Barclays Bank, Citibank, Deak Perera, Perera Express, the Republic National Bank of Dallas, and Thomas Cook – are accepted in any Russian hotel where foreigners are likely to be housed.

My traveler's checks are from American Express.
Мои туристские чеки от Америкэн Экспресс.
ma-EE too-REEST-skee-yeh CHEH-kee aht ah-MEH-ree-kehn exPRESS.

...Bank of America
...Бэнк ов Америка

...Barclays Bank
...Барклэйс Бэнк

...Citibank
...Ситибэнк

...Deak Perera
...Дик Перера

...Perera Express
...Перера Экспресс

...the Republic National Bank of Dallas
...Рипаблик Нэшинэл Бэнк ов Даллас

...Thomas Cook
...Томас Кук

CREDIT CARDS

Most major credit cards are accepted in Russia: American Express, Visa, MasterCard, Diners Club, Carte Blanche, and Eurocard. Hotels that have been accredited by Intourist (the Soviet tourist agency) and recommended to foreign visitors will accept these foreign credit cards.

I would like to exchange money from my American Express card.
Я хочу обменять деньги с моей карточки Америкэн Експресс.
ya kha-CHOO ahb-m' yeh-N'YAHT D'YEHN-gee ss ma-YEHY KAHR-tohch-kee American exPRESS.

...Visa card
...Виза

...MasterCard
...Мастеркард

...Diners Club card
...Дайнерз Клаб

MONEY

...Carte Blanche
...Карт Бланш

...Eurocard
...Юрокард

Can I change money from this card?
Могу я обменять деньги с этой карточки?
*ma-GOO ya ahb-m'yeh-N'YAHT D'YEHN-gee ss EH-ta-ee
KAHR-tahch-kee?*

Credit cards may also be used to make purchases at Intourist-approved establishments that have been recommended to foreign visitors. Some 600 hotels, restaurants, and shops in at least 60 towns and cities will accept major foreign credit cards.

Can I pay for this by credit card?
Могу я заплатить за это по кредитной карточке?
*ma-GOO ya za-pla-TEET za EH-ta pa kreh-DEET-noy
KAHR-tahch-k'yeh?*

Travelers are likely to get a better exchange rate by changing money at the official tourist rate than by making credit card purchases. However, many establishments catering to foreign visitiors will not accept roubles in payment. They may insist on payment in foreign currency, either cash, traveler's checks, or credit cards.

HARD AND SOFT CURRENCIES

Money in Russia comes in two varieties: "hard" and "soft." "Hard" currency is foreign money from capitalist countries that can be exchanged on the world market – dollars, pounds sterling, francs, Swiss francs, deutschmarks, yen, and so on. "Soft" currency is Russian currency or currency from other socialist or formerly socialist countries in the Eastern bloc. The Russian government is interested in taking in as much hard currency as possible – so that it can buy items on the world market – and money matters for foreigners are arranged accordingly.

Thus many hotels, restaurants, and shops will take only hard currency – and many other restaurants offer considerably better service, superior food, more pleasant seating, and shorter lines to customers paying in hard currency. If a hotel makes a restaurant reservation for a foreign guest, the foreigner will almost certainly be expected to pay in hard currency. Hotel-service bureaus that buy theater tickets, rent cars, obtain train or plane tickets, or place international telephone calls for visitors will expect to be paid in hard currency.

Can I pay for this in roubles?
Могу я заплатить за это в рублях?
ma-GOO ya za-pla-TEET za EH-ta v roob-L'YAHkh?

Do you take traveler's check?
Вы берете турустский чек?
vee b'yeh-R'YO-t'yeh too-REEST-skee CHEHK?

Can I pay for this with dollars?
Могу я заплатить за это в долларах?
ma-GOO ya za-pla-TEET za EH-ta v DO-la-rahkh?

...with pounds sterling?
...в фунтах стерлингов?
...f FOON-tahkh STEHR-leen-gahf?

...with French francs?
...во французских франках?
...va frahn-TSOOs-keekh FRAHN-kahkh?

...with deutschmarks?
...в немецких марках?
...v n'yeh-M'YEH-tskeekh MAHR-kahkh?

...with yen?
...в иенах?
...v ee-YEH-nahkh?

...with Swiss francs?
...в швейцарских франках?
...f shv'yeh-TSAHR-skeekh FRAHN-kahkh?

I am willing to pay with hard currency.
Я готов (готова) платить в валюте.
ya ga-TOHF (ga-TOH-va) pla-TEET v va-L'YOO-t'yeh.

MAKING PURCHASES

In addition, special tourist stores known as *beryozkas* (which means "birch trees") will only accept hard currency – in notes, traveler's checks, or credit cards. Beryozkas sell items not readily available elsewhere in Russia, as well as goods of particular interest to tourists: jewelry, amber, lacquered boxes, furs, liquor, chocolate, embroidery, wooden bowls and utensils, "matryoshka" nesting dolls, and other souvenirs.

Do you accept roubles here?
Вы принимаете рубли здесь?
vee pree-nee-MA-ee-t'yeh roob-LEE zd'yehs?

Where is the beryozka?
Где "Березка"?
gd'yeh b'yee-R'YOHZ-ka?

Establishments that specifically cater to foreign visitors will accept traveler's checks in payment, but restaurants, bars, and stores other than beryozkas prefer foreign currency or credit cards to traveler's checks. When establishments do accept traveler's checks, it is usually on the condition that they do not have to give change. Therefore, checks in small denominations are probably the most useful.

Will you accept a traveler's check?
Вы принимаете турустский чек?
vee pree-nee-MA-yeh-t'yeh too-REEST-skee check?

This is the smallest check I have.
Это самый маленький чек, который у меня есть.
EH-ta SA-mee MA-l'yehn-kee check, ka-TOH-ree oo meh-N'YA yehst.

Likewise, it is easiest to make large purchases by credit card and to make small purchases – drinks, snacks, small souvenirs – by foreign bills of smaller denominations.

Would you rather I pay by cash or by credit card?
Вы хотите, чтобы я заплатил(а) наличными или по кредитной карточке?
vee kha-TEE-t' yeh, SHTO-bee ya za-pla-TEEL(a) na-LEECH-nee-mee EE-lee pa kreh-DEET-noy KAHR-tahch-k' yeh?

Can you give change?
Вы можете разменять?
vee MO-zhee-t' yeh rahz-m' yeh-N' AHT?

Will you take a credit card for this amount?
Вы принимаете кредитную карточку на эту сумму?
vee pree-nee-MA-yeh-t' yeh kreh-DEET-noo-yoo KAHR-tahch-koo na EH-too SOOM-moo?

RELAXATION

11

BARS

The modern Soviet hotels catering to the business traveler are all equipped with bars and cocktail lounges. Bars outside of hotels serve only Russian beer, which is rationed. The bars with the best selection are the hard-currency bars inside Russian hotels, which usually serve vodka, brandy, wine, and imported spirits, as well as bottles of (non-French) champagne. Foreign travelers can also get soft drinks, mineral water, tea, and French/Italian-style coffee at hotels bars. Some Russian bars are now run as joint ventures with foreign liquor companies; these have an even wider range, but there are very few of them.

Where is the bar?
Где бар?
gd' yeh bar?

Will you join me in a drink?
Вы присоединитесь ко мне попить?
vwee pree-sa-ee-dee-NEE-t' yehs ka-mn' yeh pa-PEET?

What would you like?
Что вы хотели бы?
chto vwee kha-T'YEH-lee bee?

Day bars are open between 10 a.m. or 11 a.m. and 11 p.m. Night bars open at 11 p.m. and stay open until 4 a.m. Some bars have waiter service, but usually travelers must order over the counter. Bartenders probably won't speak much more than a few words of any language other than Russian, but will be able to convert many different currencies into roubles.

Russians usually drink vodka as part of a meal. The most popular and most easily available Soviet vodka is *stolichnaya*, although *starka* (old vodka) and *pshenichnaya* (made from wheat) can also be found. Russian wines go by number as well as name, with the most popular being Number 1, Tsinindali, a medium dry white, and Number 4, Mukuzaru, a tart red. Russian mineral water tends to taste heavy and soapy, and is used more to combat hangovers than for refreshment.

The Russian anti-alcohol campaign means that disruptive or drunken behavior in bars is subject to strong disapproval.

RELAXATION

How late is the bar open?
До скольких часов открыт бар?
da SKOHL-keekh chee-SOHF aht-kreet bar?

I'd like a glass of red wine.
Я хотел (хотела) бы стакан красного вина.
ya kha-T'YEHL (kha-T'YEH-la) bee sta-KAHN KRAHS-na-va vee-NA.

... of white wine
белого вина
B'YEH-la-va vee-NA

... of stolichnaya
столичной
sta-LEECH-noy

... of whiskey
виски
VEES-kee

... of brandy
брэнди
BREN-dee

... of champagne
шампанского
SHAHM-PAHN-ska-va

... of mineral water
минеральной воды
mee-nee-RAHL-noy va-DEE

... of tea
чаю
CHA-yoo

... of coffee
кофе
KO-f'yeh

To your health!
За ваше здоровье!
za VA-sheh zda-RO-v'yeh!

RESTAURANTS

Russian restaurants are more a place of entertainment than a chance to sample fine cuisine. Most restaurants are more geared to the needs of groups than to individuals, and many include floor shows, folk groups, dance bands, or other types of – usually loud – entertainment. Service is usually extremely slow – about 15 minutes' wait between each course and between the last course and the bill – and slows down even more during the floor show. Theatergoers don't usually attempt to eat in restaurants, but rather eat during intermission at the theater buffet.

Russian restaurants usually serve lunch from noon to 3 p.m., and reopen for dinner from 6 p.m. to 11 p.m. However, the dinner rush is between 7 p.m. and 8 p.m., and after 9 p.m., it's difficult to get served. Smoking is banned in most restaurants except for those in Intourist hotels (as a concession to foreigners). Most Russians dress up for dinner, especially if they're entertaining guests.

When do you serve lunch?
Когда вы подаете обед?
kahg-DA vee pa-da-YO-t'yeh ah-B'YEHT?

How late do you serve dinner?
До скольких часов вы подаете ужин?
da SKOHL-keekh chee-SOHF vee pa-da-YO-t'yeh OO-zheen?

We have a reservation!
У нас броня!
oo-nahs BRO-n'ya!

May I smoke?
Могу я курить?
ma-GOO ya koo-REET?

We've enjoyed visiting your restaurant!
Нам понравился ваш ресторан!
nahm pa-NRA-veel-sa vahsh rehs-ta-RAHN!

CULTURAL EVENTS

Business travelers may enjoy Russian cultural events, which may have been booked for them by their hosts. If not, the hotel service desk is usually very helpful in arranging for tickets, which are usually paid for in hard currency or by credit card. Tickets to less popular events can be bought at theater box offices or at kiosks in the city. Opera, ballet, puppet theater, and the circus are all of interest to the non-Russian-speaking visitor. Russian theater is undergoing many exciting changes, so for those who wish to brave the language barrier, a visit to a children's theater might be an interesting evening. Sporting events – usually soccer, hockey, and basketball – are popular with foreigners. Although much of interest is happening in Russian cinema today, there are few foreign-language films available in Russia.

Is there any English-language theater in this city?
В этом годоре есть ли театр на английском языке?
v' EH-tahm GO-ra-d'yeh yehst lee tee-AHTR na ahn-GLEES-kahm ya-zee-K'YEH?

Are there any English-language movies?
Есть ли фильмы по-английски?
yehst lee FEEL-mee pa-ahn-GLEES-kee?

I'd like to go to the ballet.
Я хотел (хотела) бы пойти на балет.
ya kha-T'YEHL (kha-T'YEH-la) bee pa-ee-TEE na ba-L'YEHT.

What ballets are playing?
Какие балеты в программе?
ka-KEE-yeh ba-L'YEH-tee f' pra-GRAHM-m'yeh?

Can we get tickets to the opera?
Можем мы достать билеты на оперу?
MO-zhehm mee dahs-TAHT bee-L'YEH-tee na OH-pee-roo?

Which operas are available?
Какие оперы есть?
ka-KEE yeh OH-pee-ree yehst?

I want tickets to the circus!
Я хочу билеты в цирк!
ya kha-CHOO bee-L'YEH-tee f' tseerk!

Can we go to a soccer game?
Мы можем пойти на футбольную игру?
mee MO-zheem pa-ee-TEE na foot-BOHL-noo-yoo ee-GROO?

Is there a hockey game in town?
В городе есть хоккейная игра?
v' GO-ra-d'yeh yehst kha-K'YEH-na-ya ee-GRA?

Can we see basketball?
Мы можем посмотреть баскетбол?
mee MO-zheem pahs-ma-TR'YEHT bahs-keet-BALL?

SIGHTSEEING

Sightseeing can be a pleasure in Russian cities. Foreigners used to be somewhat restricted in their taking of photographs. There should be no problem photographing regular tourist attractions, but it would be unwise to photograph any military installations, soldiers, or military equipment. Many Russian citizens do not like to be photographed, so it's most courteous to ask permission before taking a shot of anyone who is not an acquaintance.

I want to buy some film.
Я хочу купить пленку.
ya kha-CHOO koo-PEET PL'YOHN-koo.

For this camera.
Для этой камеры.
dl'ya EH-toy KA-m'yeh-ree.

Can I take photographs here?
Могу ли я сфотографировать здесь?
ma-GOO lee ya sfa-ta-gra-FEE-ra-vat zd'yehs'?

I want to photograph ...
Я хочу сфотографировать ...
ya kha-CHOO sfa-tahg-ra-FEE-ra-vaht ...

145

RELAXATION

... Red Square
Красную Площадь
KRAHS-noo-yoo PLO-sh'chaht

... the Kremlin
Кремль
kr'yehml

... an old church
старую церковь
STA-roo-yoo TSEHR-kahf

... a market
рынок
REE-nahk

MEDICINE AND HEALTH 12

Russian medical care is well up to Western standards, and foreigners who have gotten sick in Russia have reported excellent care and treatment. Although travelers who rely on either prescription or over-the-counter medication should take ample supplies with them, some Russian equivalent is probably available in case of emergency.

I want to see a doctor.
Я хочу пойти ко врачу.
ya kha-CHOO pa-ee-TEE ka vra-CHOO.

I have a cold.
Я простудился (простудилась).
ya pra-stoo-DEEL-sa (pra-stoo-DEE-las).

My throat hurts.
У меня болит горло.
oo meh-N'YA ba-LEET GOHR-la.

My head hurts.
У меня головная боль.
oo meh-N'YA ga-lahv-NA-ya bohl.

My stomach hurts.
У меня болит живот.
oo meh-N'YA ba-LEET zhee-VOHT.

My arm hurts.
У меня болит рука.
oo meh-N'YA ba-LEET roo-KA.

My leg hurts.
У меня болит нога.
oo meh-N'YA ba-LEET na-GA.

Do I have a fever?
У меня температура?
oo meh-N'YA teem-pee-ra-TOO-ra?

MEDICINE AND HEALTH

Can you give me medicine for
Вы можете дать мне лекарство от
vwee MO-zhee-t' yeh daht mn' yeh lee-KAHR-stva

...a headache?
...головной боли?
...aht ga-lahv-NOY BO-lee?

...a cold?
...простуды?
...prahs-TOO-dee?

...an upset stomach?
...расстройства желудка?
...ra-STROY-stva zhee-LOOT-ka?

I have high blood pressure.
У меня высокое кровяное давление.
oo-meh-N' YA vee-SO-ka-yeh kra-v' ya-NOY-eh dahv-L'YEH-nee-yeh.

I have a heart problem.
У меня проблема с сердцем.
oo meh-N' YA prahb-L'YEH-ma ss S'YEHR-tsehm.

Some things the doctor may say:
open your mouth
Откройте рот
aht-KROY-t' yeh roht

Inhale
Вдохните
v' dakh-nee-t' yeh

Exhale
Выдохните
vee-dakh-nee-t' yeh

Put out your tongue
Покажите язык
pa-ka-ZHEE-t' yeh ya-ZEEK

I will give you an injection.
Я сделаю вам укол.
ya sd' yeh-la-yoo vahm oo-KOHL.

– a prescription
– рецепт
– reht-sept

Take this.
Принимайте это.
pre-nee-MA-yeh-t' yee EH-ta.

Twice a day.
Два раза в день.
dva ra-ZA v' d' yen.

For minor ailments, a hotel doctor will be sent to the traveler's room. If necessary, hospitalization can be arranged in Russia, but foreign residents say that the sense of isolation caused by the language barrier makes it preferable to be hospitalized in Helsinki if at all possible. Medical services and supplies must usually be paid for in rubles, and Westerners will be surprised to see how low the prices are.

I need to go to the hospital.
Мне надо идти в больницу.
mn' yeh na-da eet-TEE v' bahl-NEE-tsoo.

Where is the hospital?
Где больница?
gd' yeh bahl-NEE-tsa?

Where is the drugstore?
Где аптека?
gd' yeh ahp-T' YEH-ka?

The most common health problems for visitors to Russia is infection with the intestinal parasite, *giardia lamblia*. This can best be avoided by drinking no tap water whatsoever. Visitors should brush their teeth with boiled or bottled water and avoid drinks with ice cubes. They might also avoid salads, fruits that cannot be peeled, and uncooked vegetables. Since fresh fruits and vegetables are in short supply in the Soviet Union, many visitors like to bring vitamin supplements with them.

Is this tap water?
Это вода из крана?
EH-ta va-DA eez KRA-na?

Is this boiled water?
Это кипеченая вода?
EH-TA kee-pee-CH'YO-na-ya va-DA?

Do you have mineral water?
У вас минеральная вода?
oo vahs mee-nee-RAHL-na-ya va-DA?

Where can I buy a bottle of water?
Где я могу купить бутылку воды?
gd'yeh ya ma-GOO koo-PEET boo-teel-KOO va-DEE?

Business travellers who need to see doctors will find them courteous and helpful. Naturally, an interpreter should be used to communicate with the doctor, but using a few phrases in Russian may also help create a friendly, cordial atmosphere.

Thank you for seeing me.
Спасибо, что вы меня приняли.
spa-SEE-ba, shto vwee meh-N'YA PREE-n'ya-LEE.

When should I come back?
Когда мне надо прийти опять?
kahk-DA mn'yeh NA-da pree-TEE ah-P'YAHT?

SHOPPING

13

Business travelers may want to take some time out of their work schedules to purchase souvenirs or gifts. Although consumer goods in Russia are in critically short supply, some products are available in the previously mentioned "Beryozka" ("birch-tree") stores, which accept only hard currency and cater only to foreigners. Jewelry, particularly amber jewelry; books, particularly children's books and art books; furs; lacquer boxes; and traditional wooden handicrafts are available at these stores.

Where is the Beryozka?
Где "Берёзка"?
gd' yeh b' yeh-R'YOZ-ka?

I want to buy ...
Я хочу купить ...
ya kha-CHOO koo-PEET ...

jewelry
драгоценности
dra-gat-SEN-nas-tee

amber
янтарь
yahn-TAHR

lacquerware
лакированные изделия
la-bee-RO-vahn-nee-yeh eez-D'YEHL-ee-ya

a present for a child
подарок для ребенка
pa-DA-rahk dl' ya r' yi-B'YON-ka

something for my wife
что-нибудь для моей жены
SHTO-nee-boot dl' ya ma-Y'EH-ee zheh-NEE

something for my husband
что-нибудь для моего мужа
SHTO-nee-BOOT dl' ya ma-y' eh-VO MOO-zha

155

SHOPPING

Department stores and local shops may make interesting tourist stops for foreign visitors, although there is likely to be very little to buy that can't be obtained for less money at home. Russian stores require standing in line three times: to select an item, to pay for the item (upon which one receives a receipt), and to pick up the item (for which one must present the receipt).

I would like to buy that.
Я хотел (хотела) бы купить это.
ya kha-T'YEHL (kha-T'YEHL-a) bee koo-PEET EH-ta.

How much is that?
Сколько это стоит?
SKOHL-ka EH-ta STO-eet?

Where do I go now?
Куда мне идти теперь?
koo-DA mn'yeh eet-TEE t'yeh-P'YEHR?

Here is my receipt.
Вот моя квитанция.
voht mah-YA kvee-TAHN-tsee-ya.

Visitors to Moscow may enjoy a trip to the Arbat, Moscow's famous shopping street, which does feature more luxury goods than anywhere else in Russia. Moscow's Ismailovo Park also features a unique flea market, or *vernissage*, during the summer months.

Where is the Arbat?
Где Арбат?
gdy'eh ahr-BAHT?

Where is the market?
Где рынок?
gd'yeh REE-nahk?

Foreign visitors who stumble upon antiques – objects made before 1945 and books published before 1966 – should know that they need export licenses to remove these goods and must pay 100% duty as well.

Is this an antique?
Это старинное произведение?
EH-ta sta-REE-na-y' eh pra-eez-v' yeh-D' YEH-nee-yeh?

Do I need an export license for this?
Мне нужно для этого разрешение на вывоз?
mn' yeh NOOZH-na dl' ya EH-ta-va rahz-r' yee-SHEY-ni-yeh na VEE-vas?

When was this made?
Когда это было изготовлено?
kahk-DA EH-ta BEE-la eez-ga-TOHV-l' yee-na?

Where was this published?
Когда это было издано?
kahk-DA EH-ta BEE-la EEZ-da-na?

DAILY LIFE AND LOCAL CUSTOMS

GIFTS

Russians are very fond of gift-giving as a means of cementing relationships and marking either a business connection or a friendship. Business visitors to Russia should bring a number of small gift items – no more than ten of each type, to avoid customs difficulties. Souvenirs of Western cities, inexpensive electronics items such as calculators or watches, pens, and books all make appropriate gifts. Scarves, silk ties, and inexpensive jewelry might be appropriate for more personal gifts if one has developed a friendship rather than simply a business relationship.

I want to give this to you.
Я хочу вам подарить это.
Ya kha-CHOO vahm pa-da-REET' EH-ta.

A small token of our friendship.
Маленький знак нашей дружбы.
MA-l'yen-kee znahk NA-shey DROOZH-bee.

This is from my home city.
Это из моего родного города.
EH-ta eez ma-ee-VO rahd-NO-va GO-ra-da.

This is a book of American art.
Это книга американского искусства.
EH-ta KNEE-ga ah-m'yeh-ree-KAHN-ska-va ees-KOOS-tva.

I'll show you how this works.
Я вам покажу, как это работает.
ya vahm pa-ka-ZHOO, kahk EH-ta ra-BO-ta-yeht.

CLIMATE

Since the former Soviet Union covers one-sixth of the world's land mass, its climate naturally varies a great deal. Buildings in cold areas are usually well-heated in winter, but the punishing outside cold leads many of the local inhabitants to wear thermal underwear simply to avoid putting on another outside layer. Any traveler going north in winter must bring covering for the head, ears, and hands as well as waterproof boots. If you travel too during the spring thaw you had better bring adequate footwear. Local inhabitants usually bring a change of shoes with them, so that they don't have to wear boots indoors. There are cloakrooms in public buildings and restaurants where outer clothing can be left; it's considered rude to continue wearing it.

Where can I change my shoes?
Где я могу переобуть туфли?
gd'yeh ya ma-GOO pyehr-yeh-o-BOOT ma-EE TOOF-lee?

Where can I leave my coat?
Где я могу оставить пальто?
gd'yeh ya ma-GOO ahs-TA-veet pahl-TOH?

Do you think it will rain today?
Вы думаете, что сегодня будет дождь?
vwee DOO-ma-ee-t'yeh shtoh see-VOHD-n'ya BOO-deet DOHZHT?

Is it supposed to snow today?
Ожидается ли, что сегодня идет снег?
ah-zhee-DA-yit-sa, shtoh s'yee-VOHD-n'ya ee-D'YOHT sn'yeg?

It's hot today.
Сегодня жарко.
see-VOHD-n'ya ZHAHR-ka.

It's cold today!
Сегодня холодно!
see-VOHD-n'ya KHO-lahd-na!

Will it get colder tonight?
Будет холоднее сегодня вечером?
BOO-d'yeht kha-lahd-N'YEH-eh s'yee-VOHD-n'ya V'YEY-chee-rahm?

Do I need an umbrella?
Мне нужен зонтик?
mn'yeh NOO-zhehn ZOHN-teek?

Should I bring a jacket?
Мне нужно принести куртку?
mn' yeh NOOZH-na pree-n' yehs-TEE KOOR-tkoo?

THINGS TO BRING WITH YOU

Toilet paper in the Soviet Union is often in short supply or of low quality by Western standards. Visitors are recommended to carry their own toilet paper with them to avoid embarrassment. Feminine hygiene products are also far below Western standards and are often not available, so women visitors are recommended to come with good supplies.

Where can I buy toilet paper?
Где я могу купить туалетную бумагу?
gd' yeh ya ma-GOO koo-PEET too-ah-L'YEHT-noo-yoo boo-MA-goo?

Where can I buy napkins?
Где я могу купить гигиенические прокладки?
gd' yeh ya ma-GOO koo-PEET gee-gee-yeh-NEE-chee-skee-yeh prah-KLAHT-kee?

CRIME

The lack of petty crime used to be one of the outstanding features of Russia, but as the market has opened up, crime has increased as well. Currently, foreign visitors are recommended not to travel after dark except in groups, not to reveal cash or valuables, and not to invite strangers into their hotel rooms (this will be discouraged by hotel personnel in any case). Violent crime, however, is virtually unknown where foreigners are concerned. If a foreigner does need help, passersby will rush to help, as will the police that can be found on every street corner. Shopkeepers or waiters may possibly make a few errors with their calculations, but they are invariably honest, and any mistakes should be treated as genuine.

Please go away.
Пожалуйста, уйдите.
pa-ZHAHL-sta, oo-ee-DEE-t' yeh.

I'm not interested.
Я не заинтересован (заинтересована).
ya n' yeh za-een-t' yeh-r' yeh-SO-van (za-een-t' yeh-r' yeh-SO-va-na).

DAILY LIFE

Can you help me?
Вы можете мне помочь?
vwee MO-zhee-t' yeh mn' yeh pa-MOHCH?

I believe you have made a mistake.
Я думаю, вы сделали ошибку.
ya DOO-ma-yoo, vwee SD'YEH-la-lee ah-SHEEP-koo.

I think that this is not the correct change.
Я думаю, это неправильная сдача.
ya DOO-ma-yoo, EH-ta nee-PRA-veel-na-ya ZDA-cha.

ADDRESSES

ADDRESSES

Note: The situation in Russia is changing so rapidly that many old organizations are dissolving, moving location, or renaming themselves. These are the most recently available addresses at time of publication.

RUSSIAN FEDERATION GOVERNMENT AGENCIES IN THE UNITED STATES

Embassy of the Russian Federation
Consular Division
1825 Phelps Place, N.W.
Washington, D.C. 20008
Tel.: 202/939-8918
Fax: 202/483-7579

Trade Representation of the Russian Federation
2001 Connecticut Avenue, N.W.
Washington, D.C. 20008
Tel.: 202/232-5988
Fax: 202/232 2917

Commercial Section
Embassy of the *U.S.S.R*
1125 16th Street, N.W.
Washington, D.C. 20036
Tel.: 202/628-7551
Fax: 202/347-5028

***Amtorg* Trading Corporation**
1755 Broadway
New York, NY 10019
Tel.: 212/956-3010

Bank for Foreign Economic Relations
(Vneshekonombank)
527 Madison Avenue
New York, NY 10022
Tel.: 212/421-8660
Fax: 212/421-8677

ADDRESSES

Belarus Machinery Inc.
Suite 1450
115 East 57th Street
New York, NY 10022
Tel.: 212/751-8550

OTHER SOURCES IN THE UNITED STATES

Russian Trade House
Horizon Square
21 Broadway
Cresskill, NJ 07626
Tel.: 201/871-7200
Fax: 201/871-7678

RUSSIAN FEDERATION GOVERNMENT AGENCIES IN OTHER COUNTRIES

Canada
The Embassy of the Russian Federation
285 Charlotte Street
Ottawa, Ontario
K1N 8L5
Canada
Tel.: 613/235-4341
Fax: 613/236-6342

The Consulate Division of the Embassy of the Russian Federation
52 Range Road
Ottawa, Ontario
K1M 8J5
Canada
Tel.: 613/236-7220
Fax: 613/238-6158

The Consulate Division of the Embassy of the Russian Federation
3655 Avenue du Musée
Montreal HCG 2E1
Canada
Tel.: 514/843-5901
Fax: 514/842-2012

United Kingdom
The Russian Federation Embassy in the United Kingdom
13 Kensington Palace Gardens
London W8 4QX
U.K.
Tel.: (44-1) 228-3628
Telex: (51) 261420

Trade Delegation of the Russian Federation in the United Kingdom
32 Highgate West Hill
Westfield
London N6
U.K.
Tel.: (44-1) 340-4492
Telex: 28577

FOREIGN EMBASSIES IN RUSSIA

United Kingdom
14 Maurice Thorez Embankment
Moscow
Tel.: 231-8511/12

Canada
23 Starokonyushenny Pereulok
Moscow
Tel: 241-5882/5070/4407

United States
19-21-23 Ulitsa Chaykovskovo
Moscow
Tel.: 252-2451/59

Commercial Counselor
U.S. Commercial Office
Office of the Agricultural Counselor
Agricultural Office of the Foreign Agricultural Service
By Mail: American Embassy,
              Moscow
              APO New York, NY 09862

Consulate General of the U.S.
15 Ulitsa Petra-Lavrova
St. Petersburg
Tel.: 292-4548
Telex: 64121527 (AMCONSUL SU)
By Mail: U.S. Consulate General St. Petersburg
              15 Box L
              APO New York, NY 09664-5440

GOVERNMENT AGENCIES IN RUSSIA

Bank for Foreign Economic Relations
(Vneshekonombank)
37 Ulitsa Plushchikha
Moscow 119121
Tel.: 246-6780, 246-6788, 246-6798
Telex: 411174, 411904, 411453

Ministry of Finance
Protocol Department
9 Ulitsa Kuibysheva
Moscow 103097
Tel.:   Foreign Relations Department, 233-4511
          Information, 298-9191

Trade and Economic Council
3 Shevchenko Embankment
Moscow
Tel.: 243-4028

Telex: 413212 (ASTEC SU)

Main Customs Administration
9 Komsomolskaya Ploshchad, 1a
Moscow 107140
Tel.:   Protocol Office, 208-2441
        Information, 208-4462

Expocentre
1a Sokolnichesky Val
Moscow 107113
Tel.: 268-5874
Telex: 411185 (EXPO SU)

Vneshekonomservice
6 Ulitsa Kuibysheva
Moscow 103735
Tel.: 925-3529
Telex: 411431 (TPP SU)

Protocol Department
Ministry of Foreign Economic Relations
32/34 Smolenskaya Sennaya
Moscow 121200
Tel.: 244-3480

Committee on Science and Technology
Ulitsa Gorkovo, 11
Moscow
Tel.: 229-2000
Telex: 411241

State Foreign Economic Commission of the
Council of Ministers
P.O. Box 9
22a Gorky Street
Moscow 103050
Tel.: 203-90000

ADDRESSES

Copyright Agency
B. Bronnaya 6A
Moscow K-104
103670
Tel.: 203-4405 or 203-5551
Fax: 200-1263
Telex: 411327 (ATVR)

Intourist
16 Marx Prospect
Moscow
Tel.: 203-6962
Telex: 411211

U.S. GOVERNMENT AGENCIES

U.S. Department of Commerce
Herbert Hoover Building
14th & Constitution Avenue N.W.
Washington D.C. 20230
Tel.: 202/482-2000
Fax: 202/482-2592

Exporter Service Staff
Bureau of Export Administration
U.S. Department of Commerce
14th & Constitution Avenue N.W.
Washington, D.C. 20230
Tel.: 202/482-4811
Fax: 202/482-3617

Office of Import Investigations
U.S. Department of Commerce
Washington, D.C. 20230
Tel.: 202/482-5050
Fax: 202/482-1059

Independent States of Commonwealth Affairs
Bureau of European Affairs
U.S. Department of State
21st & C. Street N.W.
Washington D.C. 20520
Tel.: 202/647-9370
Fax: 202/736-4710

Economic Sanctions Policy Department
Bureau of Economic Affairs
U.S. Department of State
2201 C. Street N.W.
Washington D.C. 20520
Tel.: 202/647-7489
Fax: 202/647-4064

Overseas Private Investment Corporation
1100 New York Avenue N.W.
Washington D.C. 20527
Tel.: 202/336-8400
Fax: 202/408-9859

Export-Import Bank of the United States
811 Vermont Avenue, N.W.
Washington, D.C. 20571
Tel.: 202/622-9823
Fax: 202/566-7523

U.S. Trade and Development Agency
SA-16, Room 309
Washington, D.C. 20523
Tel.: 202/875-4357
Fax: 703/875-4009

Government Printing Office
710 North Capitol Street
Washington D.C. 20402
Tel.: 202/783-3238
Fax: 202/512-2250

ADDRESSES

LEGAL SERVICES

Baker & McKenzie
Pushkin Plaza
Bolshoi Gnezdnykovsky Pereulok 7
Moscow
Tel.: 200-6167, 200-4906, 200-6186
Fax: 200-0203

Baker & McKenzie
815 Connecticut Avenue, N.W.
Washington, D.C. 20006
Tel.: 202/452-7000
Fax: 202/452-7073

BANKING SERVICES

Bank of America NT & SA, the U.S.A.
Room 1605
12 Krasnopresnenskaya Embankment
Moscow World Trade Center
Tel.: 253-7054; 253-1910; 253-1911
Telex: 413189

Chase Manhattan Bank, N.A., the U.S.A.
Room 1709
12 Krasnopresnenskaya Embankment
Moscow World Trade Center
Tel.: 230-2174; 253-1496; 253-8377
Telex: 413912

The State Bank of the *U.S.S.R.*/Gosbank *S.S.R.*
12 Neglinnaya Ulitsa
Moscow 103016
Tel.: 923-2038

**The Bank for Foreign Economic Affairs of the *U.S.S.R/*
Vneshekonombank *S.S.S.R.***
37 Ulitsa Plushchikha
Moscow 119121
Tel.: 246-6731; 227-0253

AGRICULTURAL INFORMATION

**The Foreign Agricultural Service of the United States Department
of Agriculture (USDA)**

Grains and Feed Division – Tel.: 202/447-6219

Dairy, Livestock and Poultry Division – Tel.: 202/447-8031

Oilseeds and Products Division – Tel.: 202/447-7037

Tobacco, Cotton and Seeds Division – Tel.: 202/382-9516

Horticulture and Tropical Plants Division – Tel.: 202/447-6590

The Office of Trade Policy
Africa, Asia and the Middle East Division
Foreign Agricultural Service
U.S. Department of Agriculture
Washington, D.C.
Tel.: 202/382-1289

COMMUNICATIONS SERVICES

International Telephone Exchange
(for placing calls to other countries from Moscow)
333-4101

ADDRESSES

Information
(for calls within Russia)
07

International Couriers
Barry Martin Travel
Room 940
Mezhdunarodnaya Hotel
Moscow
Tel.: 253-2940

CHAMBERS OF COMMERCE IN MOSCOW

Russian Chamber of Commerce and Industry
6 Ulitsa Kuibysheva
Moscow 103684
Tel.: 923-4323
Telex: 411126

Moscow Chamber of Commerce – Tel.: 200-7612

American–Russian Trade and Economic Council –
Tel.: 243-4028/5621/5470/5495/5228

British–Russian Chamber of Commerce – Tel.: 253-2554

Franco–Russian Chamber of Commerce – Tel.: 208-9351

Finnish–Russian Chamber of Commerce – Tel.: 925-9001

Italian–Russian Chamber of Commerce – Tel.: 241-6517

AIRLINES

Aeroflot
630 5th Avenue
New York, NY 10111
Tel.: 212/397-1660

GRAMMAR: AN INTRODUCTION & BUSINESS DICTIONARY

The following short dictionary has been prepared for business travelers in Russia and the CIS, as the former USSR is currently called. When you wish to say a word in Russian, to clarify or emphasize the short sentences in the preceding pages, simply look it up in the English word list below, followed by its Russian equivalent and then by the phonetics.

The Russian (Cyrillic) alphabet has more letters than the English one but will become easy to read through practice. Although some Russian words seem long, Russian construction is often shorter than English.

Russian nouns and adjectives comes in three genders: masculine, feminine, and neuter. Masculine nouns generally end in a consonant. Feminine nouns end in the Russian letters а, я or ь. Neuter nouns end in о or е.

Adjective endings agree with the gender of the noun: й for masculine, я for feminine and е for neuter. This short explanation is offered to make it easy for you to identify spelling changes which occur in words you may learn in the singular and then see with a different ending.

Verbs in the word list are written in the infinitive: "to see," "to hear," "to go," etc. except for the most frequently used verbs, for which several forms for person and tense are given. The infinitive usually can be recognized by ь after the verb.

These infinitives can be used with expressions like, "Do you wish to go?" "I want to see it," etc., to make basic sentences.

Verb endings in the present tense generally resemble each other.

An example:
to speak
говорить
ga-va-REET'

I speak
я говорю
ya ga-var-YOO

he (she) speaks
он (она) говорит
ohn (ah-NA) ga-va-REET

you speak
вы говорите
vwee ga-va-REET-yeh

we speak
мы говорим
mwee ga-va-REEM

they speak
они говорят
ah-NEE ga-va-YAHT

Nouns, pronouns, and adjectives have "case" endings. The nominative case is the one given in the word list and the five others are the Genitive, Dative, Accusative, Instrumental, and Prepositional cases. The cases identify their function within the sentence by their position, and the spelling of their final letters, whether they are genitive, indirect or direct object. Case endings can also indicate "with"; be a substitute for "by" or "in"; be used for comparisons and to express dimensions. They also are used after certain prepositions and verbs, and for objects following negations. The Genitive case is also used for counting numbers of objects, specifically numbers 2 to 4 and all other numbers ending in these figures.

When you use the Russian sentences in this book you do not have to worry about the right case endings as they are clearly indicated in each sentence. Their use will come to you naturally as you become familiar with the business or travel dialogue where they appear.

CYRILLIC ALPHABET

Cyrillic	English
а	ah
б	b
в	v *(pronouned "f" when ending a word)*
г	g *(pronounced "k" when ending a word)*
д	d *(pronounced "t" when ending a word)*
е	yeh or eh
ё	yo
ж	zh
з	z
и	ee
й	like "y" in "toy"
к	k
л	l
м	m
н	n
о	o (or "ah" when its syllable is *unstressed*)
п	p
р	r
с	s
т	t
у	u
ф	f
х	kh (guttural)
ц	ts
ч	ch
ш	sh
щ	sh'ch
ъ	–
ы	yee (approximately)
ь	(adds a slightly "y" sound to preceding consonants)
э	ee
ю	yoo
я	ya

DICTIONARY

a (or) one	один	*ah-DEEN*
accident	авария	*ah-VA-ree-ya*
account	счёт	*schyoht*
address	адрес	*AHD-r' yes*
administration	администрация	*ahd-mee-nee-STRA-tsee-ya*
advertisement	реклама	*ree-KLA-ma*
afternoon	вторая половина дня	*ftah-RAH-yah*
		pah-lah-VEE-na dn' yah
Africa	**Африка**	*AHF-ree-ka*
again	снова	*SNO-va*
agent	агент	*ah-GEHNT*
agree	соглашаться	*sa-gla-SHA-tsa*
agreement	соглашение	*sa-gla-SHE-nee-ye*
air conditioner	кондиционер	*kahn-dee-tsee-ah-N'YER*
air mail	авиапочта	*ah-vee-ah-POHCH-ta*
airplane	самолёт	*sa-ma-L'YOHT*
airport	аэропорт	*ah-eh-ra-PORT*
allow	разрешать	*rahz-ree-SHAHT'*
all right	**OK**	*OK*
also	также	*TAHK-zheh*
America	**Америка**	*ah-M'YE-ree-ka*
American *n.*	**американец** (m)/	*ah-m'ye-ree-KA-n'yehts/*
	американка (f)	*ah-m'ye-ree-KAHN-ka*
and	и	*ee*
answer	ответ	*aht-V'YEHT*
antibiotic	антибиотик	*ahn-tee-bee-OH-tick*
antique	старинный	*sta-REE-nee*
appliance	прибор	*pree-BORR*
appointment	встреча	*FSTR'YE-cha*
April	апрель	*ahp-R'YEHL'*
Arabian	арабский	*ah-RAHP-skee*
Armenia	**Армения**	*ahr-M'YEH-nee-ya*
arrange	устраивать	*oo-STRA-ee-vaht'*
arrangement	устройство	*oo-STROY-stva*
arrive	прибыть	*pree-BIT'*
art	искусство	*ess-KOOS-tva*
Asia	**Азия**	*AH-zee-ya*
ask	спросить	*spra-SEET'*
aspirin	аспирин	*ahs-pee-REEN*
assemble	собирать	*sa-bee-RAHT'*
at	у	*oo*
Atlantic Ocean	**Атлантический Океан**	*aht-lahn-TEE-ches-kee*
		ah-kee-AHN
attorney	юрист	*yoo-RIST*
August	август	*AHV-goost*
automobile	машина	*ma-SHEE-na*
Australia	**Австралия**	*ahf-STRA-lee-ya*

Australian *n.*	австралиец (m)/	*ahf-stra-LEE-yehts*
	австралийка (f)	*ahf-stra-LEEY-ka*
bad	плохой	*pla-KHOY*
bag	сумка	*SOOM-ka*
baggage	багаж	*ba-GAHZH*
ball point pen	шариковая ручка	*SHA-ree-ka-va-ya ROOCH-ka*
balance	баланс	*ba-LAHNS*
bank	банк	*bahnk*
banker	банкир	*bahn-KEER*
bank account	банковый счёт	*BAHN-ka-vee sch'yoht*
bank draft	банковая тратта	*BAHN-ka-vah-yah TRAHT-tah*
bargain	сделка	*SD'YEHL-ka*
bathroom	ванная	*VAHN-na-ya*
battery	батарея	*bah-tah-R'YE-yah*
basis	основа	*ahs-NO-va*
beautiful	красивый	*kra-SEE-vee*
beauty shop	косметический салон	*kahs-m'ye-TEE-ches-kee sa-LOHN*
beer	пиво	*PEE-va*
beneficiary	пользующийся	*POHL-zoo-yoosh-chee-s'yah*
best	лучший	*LOOCH-shee*
better	лучше	*LOOCH-sheh*
bicycle	велосипед	*v'ye-la-see-P'YEHT*
big	большой	*bahl-SHOY*
bill	счёт	*sch'yot*
black	чёрный	*CH'YOHR-nee*
blanket	одеяло	*ah-dee-YAH-la*
blue	голубой	*ga-loo-BOY*
boat	лодка	*LOHT-ka*
book	книга	*KNEE-ga*
borrow	взять взаймы	*vz'yaht vzaaee-MEE*
boss	босс	*boss*
box	коробка	*ka-ROHP-ka*
break	ломать	*la-MAHT'*
Briton	британец (m)/	*bree-TAHN-yehts/*
	британка (f)	*bree-TAHN-ka*
brown	коричневый	*ka-REESH-nee-vee*
build	строить	*STRO-eet'*
building	здание	*ZDA-nee-ye*
bus	автобус	*ahf-TO-boos*
business	бизнес	*business*
businessman	бизнесмен	*business man*
busy	занятый	*ZA-n'ya-tee*
but	но	*noh*
buy	покупать	*pa-koo-PAHT'*
calculator	калькулятор	*kahl-koo-L'YA-tar*

camera	фотоаппарат	foto-ahp-pa-RAHT
can (container)	банка	BAHN-ka
Canada	Канада	ka-NA-da
Canadian n.	канадец (m)/	ka-NA-d'yets/
	канадка (f)	ka-NAHT-ka
cancel	отменить	aht-m'ye-NEET'
capital (money)	капитал	ka-pee-TAHL
car	машина	mah-SHEE-na
careful	осторожный	ahs-ta-ROHZH-nee
carpet	ковёр	ka-V'YOHR
cash	наличные	na-LEECH-nee-ye
cassette tape	кассета	kahs-S'YEH-ta
catalog	каталог	ka-ta-LOG
Central Asia	Центральная Азия	tsehn-TRAHL-na-ya AH-zee-ya
ceramics	керамика	kee-RA-mee-ka
certainly	конечно	ka-N'YESH-nah
certified check	заверенный чек	za-V'YE-r'yehn-nee check
cheap	дешёвый	dee-SHOH-vee
check (bank)	чек	check
chemicals	химикаты	khee-mee-KA-tee
China	Китай	kee-TAI
Chinese n.	китаец (m)/	kee-TA-yehts/
	китаянка (f)	kee-ta-YAN-ka
choose	выбирать	vee-bee-RAHT'
city	город	GO-raht
coal	уголь	OO-gahl'
coat	пальто	pal-TOH
coffee	кофе	KOH-f'yee
commission	комиссионные	ka-mee-see-OH-nee-yeh
company	компания	kahm-PA-nee-ya
compensation	компенсация	kahm-peen-SA-tsee-ya
competition	соревнование	sa-r'yehv-na-VA-nee-ye
consignment	партия товаров	PAR-tee-yah tah-VAH-rahf
consulate	консульство	KOHN-sool-stva
cost	цена	tseh-NA
cost, insurance,	цена, страховка,	tseh-NA, stra-KHOHF-ka,
freight (C.I.F.)	груз (Ц.С.Г.)	groos (tseh-ehs-geh)
container	контейнер	kahn-T'YEY-n'yehr
container ship	контейнерный корабль	kahn-T'YEY-n'yer-nee
		ka-RAHBL'
contingency	возможное событие	vahz-MOHZH-nah-yeh
		sah-BEE-tee-yeh
contract	контракт	kahnt-RAHKT
co-operation	сотрудничество	sa-TROOD-nee-ches-tva
copy	копия	KO-pee-ya
current	текущий	tee-KOO-shchee
customer	покупатель	pah-koo-PAH-t'yehl

customs	таможня	*ta-MOHZH-n'ya*
damage	ущерб	*oo-SHCHERB*
dangerous	опасный	*ah-PAHS-nee*
date	дата	*DA-ta*
day	день	*d'yen'*
December	декабрь	*dee-KAHBR'*
delicious	вкусный	*FKOOS-nee*
deliver	доставлять	*dahs-tahv-L'YAT'*
demonstrate	демонстрировать	*de-mahn-STREE-ra-vaht'*
dentist	дантист	*dahn-TEEST*
depart	отбывать	*aht-bee-vaht'*
department store	универмаг	*oo-nee-v'yer-MAHGH*
deposit	вклад	*fklaht*
develop	развивать	*rahz-vee-VAHT'*
diesel engine	дизельный мотор	*DEE-z'yel-nee ma-TOHR*
different	другой	*droo-GOY*
difficult	трудный	*TROOD-nee*
dinner	ужин	*OO-zhin*
direction	направление	*na-prahv-L'YE-nee-yeh*
distribution	распределение	*rahs-pree-dee-L'YE-nee-yeh*
distributor	распределитель	*rahs-pree-dee-LEE-t'yehl'*
discount	скидка	*SKEET-ka*
do (perform)	делать	*D'YEH-laht'*
don't (do something)	не делать	*n'ye D'YE-laht'*
dollar	доллар	*DOHL-lahr*
dress	платье	*PLA-t'yeh*
driver	водитель	*va-DEE-t'yehl'*
drug store	аптека	*ahp-T.YEE-ka*
duty free	не подлежащий	*n'ye pahd-l'yeh-ZHAHSH-chee*
	таможенной пошлине	*tah-MOH-zhe-noy*
		POH-shlee-n'yeh
each	каждый	*KAHZH-dee*
east	восток	*vahs-TOHK*
easy	лёгкий	*L'YOKH-kee*
economy	экономия	*eh-ka-NO-mee-ya*
efficient	эффективный	*ehf-fehk-TEEV-nee*
eight	восемь	*VO-s'yehm'*
eighteen	восемьнадцать	*vo-s'yehm-NAHT-tsaht'*
eighty	восемьдесят	*VO-s'yehm-d'ye-s'yaht*
electric bulb	лампочка	*LAHM-pahch-ka*
electricity	электричество	*eel-l'yek-TREE-ches-tva*
eleven	одиннадцать	*ah-DEE-naht-tsaht'*
embassy	посольство	*pa-SOHL-stva*
emergency	крайность	*KRAAEE-nohst'*
enamel	эмаль	*ea-MAHL'*

England	**Англия**	*AHN-glee-ya*
English (language)	**английский**	*ahn-GLEE-skee*
English (person)	**англичанин** (m)/	*ahn-glee-CHA-neen/*
	англичанка (f)	*ahn-glee-CHAHN-ka*
enough	**достаточно**	*dahs-TA-tahch-na*
entire	**полный**	*POHL-nee*
entrance	**вход**	*fkhoht*
equipment	**оборудование**	*ah-ba-ROO-da-va-nee-ye*
Europe	**Европа**	*yehv-RO-pa*
evening	**вечер**	*V'YE-cher*
exchange money	**обменять деньги**	*ahb-m'ye-NYAT' D'YEN-gee*
exchange rate	**обменный курс**	*ahb-M'YEN-nee koors*
exhibition	**выставка**	*VEES-tahf-ka*
exit	**выход**	*VEE-khoht*
expedite	**ускорять**	*oos-ka-R'YAHT'*
expenses	**затраты**	*za-TRA-tee*
expensive	**дорогой**	*da-ra-GOY*
experience	**опыт**	*OH-peet*
explain	**объяснять**	*ahb-yahs-N'YAHT*
export	**экспорт**	*EX-port*
express mail	**срочная почта**	*SROHCH-na-ya POHCH-ta*
fabric	**ткань**	*tkahn'*
face	**лицо**	*lee-TSO*
factory	**фабрика**	*FAHB-ree-ka*
famous	**известный**	*eez-V'YEHST-nee*
far	**далеко**	*da-l'yeh-KO*
fashion	**мода**	*MO-da*
fast	**быстро**	*BEES-tro*
February	**февраль**	*feev-RAHL'*
fee	**плата**	*PLA-ta*
few	**несколько**	*N'YE-skahl-ka*
fifteen	**пятнадцать**	*p'ya-TNA-tsaht'*
fifty	**пятьдесят**	*p'yat-dee-S'YAHT*
film (camera)	**плёнка**	*PL'YO-nka*
final offer	**последнее предложение**	*pahs-L'YEHD-n'ye-ye*
		pree-dla-ZHEH-nee-ye
final payment	**последняя плата**	*pahs-L'YEHD-n'ya-ya PLA-ta*
finish	**кончать**	*kohn-chaht'*
firm offer	**твёрдое предложение**	*TV'YOHR-da-ye*
		preed-la-ZHEH-nee-ye
fiscal year	**финансовый год**	*fee-NAHN-sa-vee GOHT*
five	**пять**	*p'yaht'*
flashlight	**фонарь**	*fa-NAHR'*
flight	**полёт**	*pa-L'YOHT*
food	**еда**	*ye-DA*
forbidden	**запрещено**	*za-pree-shcheh-NO*

foreigner	иностранец (m)/	ee-na-STRA-n'yehts/
	иностранка (f)	ee-na-STRAHN-kah
foreign exchange	валюта	vah-L'YOO-tah
forty	сорок	SO-rahk
fourteen	четырнадцать	chee-TEER-na-tsaht'
France	Франция	FRAHN-tsee-ya
free (no cost)	бесплатный	b'yes-PLAHT-nee
freight	груз	groos
French (language)	французский	frahn-TSOO-skee
French (person)	француз (m)/	frahn-TSOOZ/
	француженка (f)	frahn-TSOO-zhehn-ka
Friday	пятница	P'YAHT-nee-tsa
friend	друг (m,f)/ подруга (f)	drook/pah-DROO-gah
from	от	oht
fur	мех	m'yekh
furniture	мебель	M'YE-b'yel'
gallon	галлон	gha-LOHN
gasoline	бензин	behn-ZEEN
gas station	бензозаправочный	b'yen-zah-zah-PRAH-vah-chnee
	пункт	punkt
German adj.	немецкий	nee-M'YEH-tskee
German n.	немец (m)/немка (f)	N'YEH-m'yehts/N'YEHM-ka
Germany	Германия	g'yer-MA-nee-ya
give	дать	daht'
glad	рад (рада)	raht (RAH-dah)
glass	стакан	sta-KAHN
go	идти	eet-TEE
gold	золото	ZO-la-ta
good-bye	до свидания	da-svee-DA-nee-ya
good morning	доброе утро	DOHB-ra-ye OOT-ra
government	правительство	pra-VEE-t'yehl-stva
gray	серый	S'YE-ree
Greece	Греция	GR'YE-tsee-ya
green	зелёный	zee-L'YO-nee
gross	валовой	va-la-VOY
guarantee	гарантировать	gah-rahn-TEE-ra-vaht'
guide	гид	gheed
half	половина	pa-la-VEE-na
he, she, it	он, она, оно	ohn, ah-NA, ah-NO
headquarters	главная контора	GLAHV-na-ya kahn-TOO-rah
hear	слушать	SLOO-shaht'
heavy	тяжёлый	t'ya-ZHO-lee
help (assist)	помочь	po-MOHCH'
here	здесь	zd'yehs'

high	высокий	vee-SO-kee
hire	нанимать	na-nee-MAHT'
holiday	праздник	PRAHZ-dneek
Holland	Голландия	gah-LAHN-dee-ya
hospital	больница	bahl' NEE-tsa
host	хозяин	kha-Z'YA-een
hotel	гостиница	gahs-TEE-nee-tsa
hour	час	chahs
how	как	kahk
how are you?	как дела?	kahk d' yeh-LA
how does it work?	как это работает?	kahk EH-ta ra-BO-ta-yeht
how far?	как далеко?	kahk da-l' yeh-KO
how long?	как долго?	kahk DOHL-ga
how much?	сколько?	SKOHL'-ka
hundred	сто	sto
hundred thousand	сто тысяч	STO-TEE-s' yahch
hurry	спешить	spee-SHEET'
husband	муж	moozh
I	я	ya
ice	лёд	l' yoht
icon	икона	ee-KO-na
if	если	YEH-slee
immediately	немедленно	ne-M'YEHD-l' yehn-na
import	импорт	EEM-port
import license	разрешение на ввоз	rahz-r' yeh-SHEH-nee-yeh nah VVOHS
important	важный	VAHZH-nee
impossible	невозможный	nee-vahz-MOHZH-nee
in	в	v'
income	доход	da-KHOHT
income tax	подоходный налог	pa-da-KHOHD-nee na-LOHK
India	Индия	India
industry	промышленность	pra-MEE-shl' yee-nahst'
inexpensive	недорогой	nee-da-ra-GOY
information	информация	een-for-MA-tsee-ya
insurance	страховка	stra-KHO-vka
installment	очередной взнос	ah-chee-reed-NOY vznohs
interest (payment)	проценты	prah-TSEN-tee
interpreter	переводчик	peh-reh-VOHT-chick
investment	вложение	vla-ZHEH-nee-ye
invoice	накладная	na-kla-DNA-ya
iron (metal)	железо	zhee-L'YEH-za
Israel	Израиль	ezz-RA-eel'
Italy	Италия	ee-TA-lee-ya
jacket	пиджак	peed-ZHAHK

January	январь	*yahn-VAHR'*
Japan	Япония	*ya-PO-nee-ya*
Japanese *adj.*	японский	*ya-POHN-skee*
Japanese (person)	японец (m)/японка (f)	*ya-PO-n'yets/ya-POHN-ka*
Jew	еврей (m)/еврейка (f)	*yehv-REY/yehv-REY-ka*
jewelry	драгоценности	*drah-gah-TSEN-nahs-tee*
joint venture	совместное	*sahv-M'YE-stna-ye*
	предприятие	*preet-pree-YA-te-ye*
July	июль	*ee-YOOL'*
keep	хранить	*khra-NEET'*
key	ключ	*kl'yooch*
kilogram	килограмм	*kee-la-GRAHM*
kilometer	километр	*kee-la-M'YEHTR*
know	знать	*znaht'*
Korea	Корея	*ka-REH-ya*
Korean *n.*	кореец (m)/	*ka-REH-yehts/*
	корейка (f)	*ka-REH-ka*
Korean *adj.*	корейский	*ka-REH-skee*
lacquer	лак	*lahk*
late	поздно	*POHZ-dna*
later	позже	*POHZH-zheh*
lavatory	туалет	*too-ah-L'YEHT*
law	закон	*za-KOHN*
lawyer	юрист	*yoo-RIST*
leather	кожа	*KO-zha*
leave	уезжать	*oo-yehzh-ZHAHT'*
left	левый	*L'YE-vee*
legal	законный	*za-KOHN-nee*
length	длина	*dlee-NA*
Let's go!	пойдём!	*pa-eed-YOHM!*
letter	письмо	*pees-MO*
letter of credit	аккредитив	*ahk-kr'yeh-dee-TEEF*
(irrevocable)	безвозвратрый	*b'yehz-vahz-VRAHT-nee*
license (car)	права	*pra-VA*
(a) little bit	немного	*nee-MNO-ga*
little (small)	маленький	*MA-l'yehn-kee*
list	список	*SPEE-sahk*
listen	слушать	*SLOO-shaht'*
loan	давать взаймы	*da-VAHT' vzai-MEE*
local	местный	*M'YEHST-nee*
location	расположение	*rahs-pa-la-ZHEN-nee-ye*
long life..!	на здоровье!	*na zda-RO-v'yeh!*
loss	потеря	*pa-T'YEH-r'ya*
lost and found office	бюро находок	*b'yoo-RO na-KHOH-dak*

DICTIONARY

luck (bad)	неудача	*n' yeh-oo-DA-cha*
good luck!	желаю успеха	*zhee-LAH-yoo oo-SP'YEH-kha!*
lunch	обед	*ah-B'YEHT*
machine	машина	*ma-SHEE-na*
made in...	изготовлено в...	*eez-gah-TOHV-l' yee-na v...*
mail	почта	*PONCH-ta*
(to) make	делать	*d'YEH-laht'*
manager	менеджер	*MEN-neh-jer*
(to) manufacture	производить	*pra-eez-va-DEET'*
many	много	*MNO-ga*
map	карта	*KAR-ta*
March	март	*mart*
market	рынок	*REE-nahk*
married (m)	женатый	*zheh-NA-tee (m)*
(f)	замужняя	*za-MOOZH-n' ya-ya (f)*
material	материал	*ma-t' yeh-ree-YAHL*
May I?	Могу ли я?	*ma-GOO lee ya?*
May	май	*maaee*
maybe	может быть	*MO-zhet beet'*
me	меня	*men-YA*
to me	мне	*mn' yeh*
with me	со мной	*sa mnoy*
meat	мясо	*M'YA-sa*
mechanic	механик	*meh-KHA-nek*
medicine	лекарство	*l' yee-KAR-stva*
(Happy to) meet you!	очень рад (рада)	*OH-chehn raht (RAH-da)*
menu	меню	*meh-n' yoo*
message	сообщение	*sah-ahpsh-CHEY-nee-yeh*
milk	молоко	*ma-la-KO*
million	миллион	*mee-lee-YOHN*
mineral	минерал	*mee-neh-RAHL*
minute	минута	*mee-NOO-ta*
mistake	ошибка	*ah-SHEEP-ka*
misunderstanding	недоразумение	*n' yeh-dah-rah-zoo-MEN-ee-yeh*
model	модель	*ma-DEHL*
Monday	понедельник	*pa-n' yeh-D'YEHL'-nik*
money	деньги	*D'YEHN'-gee*
month	месяц	*M'YEH-s'yahts*
morning	утро	*OOT-rah*
mother	мать	*maht'*
motor	мотор	*ma-TOR*
motorcycle	мотоцикл	*ma-ta-TSEEKL*
movies	кино	*kee-NO*
much	много	*MNO-gah*
museum	музей	*moo-Z'YEH*
music	музыка	*MOO-zee-ka*

name	имя	*EEM-ya*
narrow	узкий	*OOS-kee*
near	близко	*BLEES-ka*
necessary	необходимо	*n' yeh-ab-kha-DEE-ma*
(I) need	мне нужно	*mn' yeh NOOZH-na*
we need	нам нужно	*nahm NOOZH-na*
net weight	чистый вес	*CHEE-stee v' yess*
never	никогда	*nee-kahg-DA*
never mind!	ничего!	*nee-cheh-VO!*
new	новый	*NO-vee*
news	новости	*NO-va-stee*
newspaper	газета	*ga-Z'YEH-ta*
next	следующий	*SL'YEH-doo-yoosh-chee*
night	ночь	*nohch*
nine	девять	*D'YEH-v' yaht*
nineteen	девятнадцать	*d' yeh-v' yaht-NAHT-tsaht*
ninety	девяносто	*d' yeh-v' ya-NOH-sta*
no	нет	*n' yet*
nobody	никто	*neek-TOH*
noise	шум	*shoom*
noon	полдень	*POHL-d' yen'*
north	север	*S'YEH-vehr*
not	не	*n' yeh*
not yet	ещё нет	*yesh-CHO n'yet*
nothing	ничего	*nee-chee-VO*
November	ноябрь	*na-YAHBR'*
now	сейчас	*s' yey-CHAS*
nowhere	нигде	*nee-GD'YEH*
number	номер	*NO-mehr*
occupied	занятый	*ZAHN-ya-tee*
ocean	океан	*ah-keh-AHN*
October	октябрь	*ahk-T'YAPR'*
(to) offer	предлагать	*pred-la-GAHT'*
office	оффис	*OH-fees*
officer	офицер	*ah-fee-TSER*
official *adj.*	официальный	*ah-fee-tsee-AHL' -nee*
often	часто	*CHA-sta*
oil	масло	*MA-sla*
O.K.	хорошо	*kha-ra-SHO*
once	однажды	*ahd-NAHZH-dee*
only	только	*TOL'-ka*
open	открыто	*aht-KREE-ta*
(to) open	открывать	*aht-kree-VAHT'*
opportunity	возможность	*vahz-MOHZH-nast'*
opposite	напротив	*na-PRO-teef*
or	или	*EE-lee*

191

DICTIONARY

orange (fruit)	апельсин	*ah-p'yel'-SEEN*
orchestra	оркестр	*ahr-K'YESS-tr*
order (business)	заказ	*za-KAHS*
(to) order	заказывать	*za-KA-zee-ee-vaht'*
in order to	чтобы	*SHTOH-bee*
other	другой	*droo-GOY*
our	наш (наша, наше)	*nahsh (NA-sha, NA-sheh)*
outside	снаружи	*sna-ROO-zhee*
over	через	*CHEH-rez*
(to) owe	быть должным	*beet DOHLZH-neem*
(to) own	владеть	*vla-D'YEHT'*
owner	владелец (m)/	*vla-D'YEH-l'yehts/*
	владелица (f)	*vlah-D'YEH-lee-tsah*
(to) pack	паковать	*pa-ka-VAHT'*
paid	оплачено	*ah-PLA-cheh-na*
pain	боль	*bohl'*
(to) paint	красить	*KRA-seet'*
painting	картина	*kar-TEE-na*
palace	дворец	*dva-R'YETS*
paper	бумага	*boo-MA-ga*
(to) park	ставить на стоянку	*STAH-veet' nah stah-YAHN-ky*
park	парк	*park*
part	часть	*chahst'*
partner	партнер	*part-N'YOR*
passenger	пассажир	*pa-sa-ZHEER*
passport	паспорт	*PAHS-port*
(to) pay	платить	*pla-TEET'*
peace	мир	*meer*
pen (fountain)	авторучка	*ahf-tah-ROOCH-kah*
pencil	карандаш	*ka-rahn-DAHSH*
people (pl.)	люди	*L'YOO-dee*
percent	процент	*pra-TSENT*
perfect	отличный	*aht-LEECH-nee*
perfume	духи	*doo-HEE*
perhaps	возможно	*vahs-MOHZH-na*
permit	разрешение	*rahz-reh-SHE-nee-yeh*
permitted	разрешено	*rahz-r'yeh-sheh-NO*
person	человек	*cheh-la-VEK*
photograph *n.*	фотография	*fo-ta-GRA-fee-ya*
(to) photograph	фотографировать	*fo-ta-gra-FEE-roh-vat'*
picture	картина	*kar-TEE-na*
pill	таблетка	*tahb-L'YET-ka*
pillow	подушка	*pa-DOOSH-ka*
place	место	*M'YES-ta*
plan	план	*plahn*
plane (airplane)	самолёт	*sa-ma-L'YOHT*

planet	планета	*pla-N'YEH-ta*
plant (factory)	завод	*za-VOHT*
plate	тарелка	*ta-R'YEL-ka*
(to) play	играть	*ee-GRAHT'*
pleasant	приятный	*pree-YAHT-nee*
Please!	пожалуйста!	*pa-ZHAHL-stah*
poem	поэма	*pah-EH-mah*
Poland	Польша	*POHL'-sha*
Pole *n.*	поляк (m)/полька (f)	*pahl'-YAHK/POHL'-ka*
police	милиция	*mee-LEE-tsee-ya*
Polish	польский	*POHL'-skee*
polite	вежливый	*VEZH-lee-vee*
politics	политика	*pa-LEE-tee-ka*
poor	бедный	*B'YED-nee*
pork	свинина	*zvee-NEE-na*
port	порт	*port*
possible	возможно	*vahz-MO-zhna*
postcard	открытка	*aht-KREET-ka*
post office	почта	*POHCH-ta*
potato	картошка	*kat-TOSH-ka*
(to) prefer	предпочитать	*pret-pa-chee-TAHT'*
premium	премия	*PREH-mee-ya*
(to) prepare	приготовлять	*pree-ga-TOH-vlyat'*
president	президент	*preh-zee-D'YENT*
(to) press (clothes)	гладить	*GLA-deet'*
price	цена	*tseh-NA*
priest	священник	*sv'ya-SH'CHEN-nik*
prison	тюрьма	*t'yoor'-MA*
private	частный	*CHAHST-nee*
probably	вероятно	*v'ye-rah-YAHT-nah*
problem	проблема	*pra-BL'YEH-ma*
production	производство	*pra-eez-VOHT-stva*
profession	профессия	*pra-F'YES-see-ya*
professor	профессор	*pra-FES-sor*
profit	прибыль	*PREE-beel'*
program	программа	*pra-GRAHM-ma*
(to) promise	обещать	*ah-b'yeh-SH'CHAHT'*
property	владение	*vla-D'YEH-nee-yeh*
public	публика	*POOB-lee-ka*
publisher	пздатель	*eez-DA-t'yel'*
(to) pull	тянуть	*T'YA-noot'*
(to) push	толкать	*tahl-KAT'*
I put	я кладу	*(ya) kla-DOO*
you put	вы кладёте	*(vwee) kla-d'YO-t'yeh*
quality	качество	*KA-chest-va*
quantity	количество	*ka-LEE-chest-va*

DICTIONARY

question	вопрос	*va-PROHS*
quickly	быстро	*BEE-stra*
quiet	спокойно	*spa-KOY-na*
quite	совершенно	*sa-ver-SHEN-na*
race (contest)	гонка	*GOHN-ka*
radio	радио	*RA-deo*
railroad	железная дорога	*zheh-L'YEZ-na-ya da-RO-ga*
raincoat	плащ	*plahsh'-ch*
rain	дождь	*doshd'*
rarely	редко	*R'YET-ka*
rat	крыса	*KREE-sa*
rate (of exchange)	курс	*koorss*
(to) read	читать	*chee-TAHT*
ready (finished)	готовый	*ga-TOH-vee*
real	реальный	*reh-AHL'-nee*
receipt	квитанция	*kvee-TAHN-tsee-yah*
(to) receive	получать	*a-loo-CHANT*
recently	недавно	*n'yeh-DA-vna*
(to) recognize	узнавать	*oo-zna-VAHT*
(to) recommend	рекомендовать	*reh-ko-men-da-VAHT*
red	красный	*KRA-snee*
refrigerator	холодильник	*kha-la-DEEL'-nik*
(to) refuse	отказывать	*aht-KA-zee-vaht'*
My regards to…	передайте	*p'yeh-r'yeh-DAHEE-t'yeh*
	мой привет …	*moy pree-V'YEHT*
(to) remain	оставаться	*ah-sta-VAHT-s'ya*
(to) remember	помнить	*POHM-neet'*
(to) rent	снимать	*snee-MAHT'*
(to) repair	ремонтировать	*reh-mahn-TEE-ra-vaht'*
(to) repeat	повторять	*pa-f'tah-R'YAHT*
report	доклад	*da-KLAHT*
representative	представитель	*prehd-sta-VEE-t'yel'*
responsible	ответственный	*aht-V'YETST-veh-nee*
restaurant	ресторан	*res-ta-RAHN*
(to) restrict	ограничивать	*ah-gra-NEE-chee-vaht'*
(to) return	возвращаться	*voz-vra-SHCHA-t'sya*
revolution	революция	*reh-va-L'YOO-tsee-ya*
reward	награда	*na-GRA-da*
rich	богатый	*ba-GA-tee*
(to) ride (in a vehicle)	ездить	*YEZ-deet'*
rifle (gun)	винтовка	*ven-TOHF-ka*
right (correct)	правильно	*PRA-veel'-na*
right (direction)	направо	*na-PRA-va*
Right away!	сразу!	*ZRA-zoo!*
ring (jewelry)	кольцо	*kahl'-TSO*
river	река	*r'yeh-KA*

road	дорога	da-RO-ga
room	комната	KOHM-na-ta
route	маршрут	marsh-ROOT
rug	ковёр	ka-V'YOR
(to) run	бежать	bee-ZHAHT'
Russia	россия	ra-SEE-ya
Russian *n.*	россиянин (m)/	rahs-see-YAH-neen/
	россиянка (f)	rahs-see-YAHN-kah
in Russian	по-русски	pa-ROO-skee
safely	безопасно	b' yeh-za-PA-sna
salad	салат	sa-LAHT
salary	жалованье	ZHAH-lah-vah-n' yeh
salesman	продавец	pra-da-V'YETS
same	тот же самый	toht zhe SA-mee
sandwich	бутерброд	boo-ter-BROHT
Saturday	суббота	soo-BO-ta
sausage	колбаса	kahl-ba-SA
(to) say	говорить	ga-va-REET'
school	школа	SHKO-la
science	наука	na-OO-ka
scissors	ножницы	NOHZH-nee-tsee
sea	море	MO-r' yeh
seat	место	M'YES-ta
secretary	секретарь (m)/	seh-kreh-TAR'/
	секретарша (f)	seh-kreh-TAR-sha
(to) see	видеть	VEE-d' yeht'
seldom	редко	R'YET-ka
(to) sell	подавать	pra-da-VAHT'
(to) send	посылать	pa-see-LAHT'
(to) separate	разделять	rahz-d' yeh-L'YAHT'
September	сентябрь	sen-T'YABR'
serious	серьёзный	s' yer-YOHZ-nee
seven	семь	s' yem
seventeen	семнадцать	s' yem-NAHT-tsaht'
seventy	семьдесят	S'YEM-d' yeh-s' yaht
several	несколько	N'YEH-skahl'-ka
sharp	острый	OH-stree
she	она	ah-NA
ship	корабль	ka-RAHBL'
(to) ship (merchandise)	отравлять	aht-prahv-L'YAHT'
shipment	груз товара	GROOZ tah-VAH-rah
shirt	рубашка	roo-BA-shka
shoe	полуботинок	pah-loo-bah-TEE-nahk
shop	магазин	na-ga-ZEEN
short	короткий	ka-ROHT-kee
shortage	нехватка	n' yekh-VAHT-ka

DICTIONARY

(to) show	показывать	*pa-KA-zee-vaht'*
show me ...	покажите мне ...	*pa-ka-ZHEE-t' yeh mn' yeh ...*
shower	душ	*doosh*
(to) shut	закрывать	*za-kree-VAHT'*
sick	больной	*bahl'-NOY*
silver	серебро	*s' yeh-r' yeh-BRO*
simple	простой	*pra-STOY*
sincere	искренний	*EES-kr' yen-nee*
(to) sing	петь	*p' yet'*
sister	сестра	*s' yeh-STRA*
(to) sit	сидеть	*see-D' YET'*
Sit down!	садитесь!	*sa-DEET-yes'!*
six	шесть	*shest*
sixteen	шестнадцать	*shest-NAHT-t' saht'*
sixty	шестьдесят	*shes-d' yeh-S' YAHT*
size	размер	*rahz-M' YEHR*
skirt	юбка	*YOOP-ka*
(to) sleep	спать	*spaht'*
slowly	медленно	*M' YED-len-na*
small	маленький	*MA-l' yen-kee*
(to) smoke	курить	*koo-REET'*
snow	снег	*sn' yek*
so	так	*tahk*
soap	мыло	*MEE-la*
socks	носки	*na-SKEE*
soft	мягкий	*M' YAKH-kee*
soldier	солдат	*sahl-DAHT*
some (a little)	немного	*n' yeh-MNO-ga*
somebody	кто-нибудь	*K' TOH-nee-boot'*
something	что-нибудь	*SHTOH-nee-boot'*
sometimes	иногда	*ee-nahg-DA*
somewhere	где-нибудь	*G' D' YEH-nee-boot'*
son	сын	*sin*
song	песня	*P' YES-n' ya*
soon	скоро	*SCORE-ah*
(I am) sorry	я сожалею	*(ya) sa-zha-L' EH-yoo*
soup	суп	*soup*
south	юг	*yuke*
South America	Южная Америка	*YOOZH-na-ya ah-MEH-ree-ka*
South American	южноамериканский	*YOOZH-na-ah-mer-ree-KAHN-skee*
Spain	Испания	*ee-SPA-nee-ya*
Spaniard	испанец (m)/	*ee-SPA-n' yets'/*
	испанка (f)	*ee-SPAHN-ka*
Spanish	испанский	*ee-SPAHN-skee*
(to) speak	говорить	*ga-va-REET'*
special	специальный	*spetz-YAHL-nee*
(to) spend	тратить	*TRA-teet'*

spoon	ложка	*LOZH-ka*
sport	спорт	*sport*
spring (season)	весна	*vehss-NA*
stairs	лестница	*L'YES-neet-sa*
stamp (postage)	почтовая марка	*pah-CHTOH-vah-yah MAR-ka*
star	звезда	*zv'yez-DA*
(to) start	начинать	*na-chee-NAHT'*
steak	бифштекс	*beef-SHTEKS*
station (train)	станция	*STAHN-tsee-ya*
(to) stay	оставаться	*ah-sta-VAHT-s'ya*
steel	сталь	*stahl*
stone	камень	*KA-mehn'*
Stop!	оснановитесь!	*ah-sta-na-VEE-t'yes!*
(a) stop (bus, etc.)	остановка	*ah-sta-NOHF-ka*
store	магазин	*ma-ga-ZEEN*
Straight ahead!	прямо	*PR'YA-ma!*
street	улица	*OO-leet-sa*
student	студент (m)/	*stoo-D'YENT'/*
	студентка (f)	*stoo-D'YENT-ka*
(to) study	учиться	*oo-CHEET-sa*
style	стиль	*steel'*
subway	метро	*meh-TRO*
such	такой	*ta-KOY*
suddenly	вдруг	*v'drook*
sugar	сахар	*SA-khar*
suit (clothes)	костюм	*ka-ST'YOOM*
summer	лето	*L'YEH-ta*
sun	солнце	*SOHN-tseh*
Sunday	воскресенье	*va-skreh-S'YEH-nee-yeh*
supervisor	надзиратель	*nahd-zee-RAH-t'yel'*
Swede	швед (m)/	*shv'yet/*
	шведка (f)	*shv'YET-ka*
Sweden	Швеция	*SHVEH-tsee-ya*
sweet	сладкий	*SLAHT-kee*
(to) swim	плавать	*PLA-vaht'*
table	стол	*stohl*
(to) take	брать	*braht'*
tall	высокий	*vwee-SO-kee*
tape	плёнка	*PL'YOHN-ka*
tape recorder	магнитофон	*mahg-nee-ta-FOHN*
tax	налог	*na-LOHK*
taxi	такси	*tahk-SEE*
tea	чай	*chaaee*
(to) teach	учить	*oo-CHEET'*
teacher	учитель (m)/	*oo-CHEET-yel'/*
	учительница (f)	*oo-CHEET-yel'-nee-tsa*

197

team	команда	*ka-MAHN-da*
telegram	телеграмма	*teh-leh-GRA-ma*
telephone	телефон	*teh-leh-FOHN*
television	телевидение	*teh-leh-VEE-dee-nee-yeh*
(to) tell	сказать	*ska-ZAHT'*
Tell her	скажите ей	*ska-ZHEET-yeh yay*
Tell him	скажите ему	*ska-ZHEET-yeh yeh-MOO*
Tell me	скажите мне	*ska-ZHEET-yeh mn' yeh*
ten	десять	*D'YEH-s'yaht*
terrible	ужасный	*oo-ZHAHS-nee*
than	чем	*chem*
(to) thank	благодарить	*bla-ga-da-REET'*
Thank you!	спасибо!	*spa-SEE-ba!*
that (one)	тот	*toht*
that (dem.)	тот (m), та (f), то (n)	*toht (m), ta (f), toh (n)*
that (rel.)	котоый (m)/	*ka-TO-ree (m)/*
	которая (f)/	*ka-TO-ra-ya (f)/*
	которое (n)	*ka-TO-ra-yeh (n)*
theater	театр	*tee-AHTR*
their, them	их	*eekh*
then	тогда	*tahg-DA*
there	там	*tahm*
therefore	поэтому	*pa-EH-ta-moo*
these	эти	*EH-tee*
they	они	*ah-NEE*
thin	тонкий	*TOHN-kee*
thing	вещь	*v'yesh'ch*
(to) think	думать	*DOO-maht'*
thirteen	тринадцать	*tree-NAHT-saht'*
thirty	тридцать	*TREET-saht'*
this	это	*EH-ta*
those	те	*t'yeh*
thousand	тысяча	*TEE-seh-cha*
three	три	*tree*
Thursday	четверг	*chet-V'YERK*
tire (auto)	шина	*SHEE-na*
tired	устал (m)/	*oo-STAHL/*
	устала (f)	*oo-STA-la*
to (direction)	к, ко	*k', ka*
to (in order to)	чтобы	*SHTO-bee*
today	сегодня	*s'yeh-VOHD-n'ya*
toilet	туалет	*twa-LET*
tomorrow	завтра	*ZAHF-tra*
tomorrow morning	завтра утром	*ZAHF-tra OO-trahm*
tomorrow night	завтра вечером	*ZAHF-tra V'YEH-cheh-rahm*
tonight	сегодня вечером	*s'yeh-VOHD-n'ya*
		V'YEH-cheh-rahm

too (also)	тоже	*TOH-zheh*
too (excessive)	слишком	*S'LEESH-kahm*
tour	поездка	*pa-YEZD-ka*
towel	полотенце	*pa-la-T'YEN-tseh*
town	город	*GO-raht*
toy	игрушка	*ee-GROOSH-ka*
trade fair	торговая выставка	*tar-GO-va-ya VEE-stahf-ka*
train	поезд	*PO-yest*
translation	перевод	*peh-r'yeh-VOHT*
(to) travel	путешествовать	*poo-teh-SHEST-va-vaht'*
treasurer	казначей	*kahz-na-CHEY*
trip	путешествие	*poo-teh-SHEST-vee-yeh*
trouble	беспокойство	*b'yes-pa-KOY-stva*
truck	грузовик	*groo-za-VEEK*
truth	правда	*PRAHV-da*
(to) try (attempt)	пробовать	*PRO-ba-vaht'*
Tuesday	вторник	*F'TOR-nik*
Turkey	Турция	*TOOR-tsee-ya*
Turkish (adj.)	турецкий	*too-RETS-kee*
Turk	турок (m)/	*TOO-rahk/*
	турчанка (f)	*toor-CHAHN-ka*
twelve	двенадцать	*dvee-NAHT-saht'*
twenty	двадцать	*DVA-tsaht'*
two	два	*dva*
typewriter	пишущая машинка	*PEE-shoosh-cha-ya*
		ma-SHEEN-ka
typist	машинистка (f)	*ma-shee-NEEST-ka*
Ukraine	Украина	*oo-kra-EE-na*
Ukrainian	украинец (m)/	*oo-kra-EE-n'yets/*
	украинка (f)	*oo-kra-EEN-ka*
umbrella	зонтик	*ZOHN-teek*
uncultured	некультурный	*n'yeh-kool'-TOOR-nee*
under	под	*poht*
(to) understand	понимать	*pa-nee-MAHT'*
Do you understand?	вы понимаете?	*vwe pa-nee-MA-yeh-t'yeh?*
I don't understand.	я не понимаю	*ya n'yeh pa-nee-MA-yoo.*
uniform	форма	*FOR-ma*
union	союз	*sa-YOOS*
United Nations	Объединенные	*ahb-yeh-dee-N'YOHN-nee-yeh*
	нации	*NA-tsee*
United States	Соединенные Штаты	*sa-yeh-deen-YO-nee-yeh*
		SH'TA-tee
university	университет	*oo-nee-veer-see-T'YENT*
unlawful	незаконный	*n'yeh-za-KOHN-nee*
until	до	*da*
up	вверх	*v'verkh*

DICTIONARY

urgent	срочный	S'ROHCH-nee
us, to us	нас, нам	nahs, nahm
(to) use	использовать	eez-POHL-za-vaht'
useful	полезный	pa-L'YEZ-nee
usual	обычный	ah-BEECH-nee
vacant	свободный	sva-BOHD-nee
vacation	каникулы	ka-NEE-koo-lee
vaccination	прививка	pree-VEEF-ka
value	ценность	TSEHN-nost'
various	различный	raz-LEECH-nee
very	очень	OH-chen'
very good	очень хорошо	OH-chen ha-ra-SHO
view	вид	veet
village	деревня	d'yeh-R'YEV-n'ya
(to) visit	посещать	pa-s'yeh-SH'CHAT'
Volga	Волга	VOHL-ga
voyage	путешествие	poo-teh-SHEST-vee-eh
(to) wait	ждать	zh'daht'
waiter	официант/	ah-fee-tsee-AHNT/
waitress	официантка	ah-fee-tsee-AHNT-ka
(to) walk	идти пешком	eet-TEE p'yesh-KOM
wallet	бумажник	boo-MAHZH-nik
(to) want	хотеть	ha-T'YET'
(I) want	я хочу	ya ha-CHOO
he (she) wants	он (она) хочет	ohn (ah-NA) HO-chet
we want	мы хотим	mwee ha-TEEM
you want	вы хотите	vwee ha-TEET-yeh
they want	они хотят	ah-NEE ha-T'YAHT
Do you want..?	вы хотите..?	Vwee ha-TEET-yee..?
war	война	voy-NA
(I) was	я был	ya bweel
he was, she was	он был, она была	ohn-bweel, ah-NA bwee-LA
it was	оно было	ah-NO BWEE-la
watch (timepiece)	часы	cha-SEE
(to) watch	смотреть	sma-TR'YET'
Watch out!	Будьте внимательны!	BOOT-t'yeh vnee-MA-tel-nee!
water	вода	va-DA
way	путь	poot'
we	мы	mwee
weak	слабый	SLA-bee
(to) wear	носить	na-SEET'
weather	погода	pa-GO-da
Wednesday	среда	sreh-DA
week	неделя	neh-D'YEH-l'ya
weight	вес	v'yes

Welcome!	Добро пожаловать!	*DOH-bra pa-ZHA-la-vaht'!*
You are welcome!	Пожалуйста	*pa-ZHAHL-sta!*
he (she, it) went	он ушёл, (она ушла), (оно ушло)	*ohn oo-SHOHL, (ah-NA oo-SHLA), (ah-NO oo-SHLO)*
you (we, they) went	вы (мы, они) ушли	*vwee (mwee, ah-NEE) oo-SHLEE*
you (we, they) were	вы (мы, они) были	*vwee (mwee, ah-NEE) BWEE-lee*
west	запад	*ZA-paht*
what	что	*shtoh*
What's the matter?	в чём дело?	*f'ch'yom D'YEH-la?*
What time is it?	который час?	*ka-TOH-ree chahs?*
At what time?	в котором часу?	*f'ka-TOH-rahm chahs-SOO?*
when?	когда?	*kahg-DA?*
where?	куда?	*koo-DA?*
which	который	*ka-TOH-ree*
while	пока (also "so long!")	*pa-KA*
white	белый	*B'YEH-lee*
who?	кто?	*k'toh?*
whom?	кого?	*ka-VO?*
whose?	чей?	*chey?*
why?	почему?	*pa-cheh-MOO?*
wide	широкий	*shee-RO-kee*
wife	жена	*zheh-NA*
(I) will	я буду	*ya BOO-doo*
he (she, it) will	он (она, оно) будет	*ohn (ah-NA, ah-NO) BOOD'yet*
we will	мы будем	*(mwee BOOD-d'yem,*
you will	вы будете	*vwee BOOD-yet-t'yeh*
they will	они будут	*ah-NEE BOO-doot)*
(to) win	выигрывать	*vwee-EE-gree-vaht'*
winter	зима	*zee-MA*
wish	желание	*zheh-LA-nee-yeh*
(to) wish	желать	*zheh-LAHT'*
with	с	*s'*
without	без	*b'yez*
wolf	волк	*vohlk*
woman	женщина	*ZHENSH-chee-na*
word	слово	*SLO-va*
work	работа	*ra-BO-ta*
(to) work	работать	*ra-BO-taht'*
world	мир	*meer*
Don't worry!	не волнуйтесь!	*n'yeh vahl-NOO-yeh-t'yes!*
Would you like..?	хотите ли вы..?	*ha-TEET-yeh lee vwee..?*
I would like…	я хотел бы… (я хотела бы)	*ya ha-T'YEL bwee … (ya ha-T'YE-la bwee…)*
(to) write	писать	*pee-SAHT'*
Write it!	напишите это!	*na-pee-SHEE-t'yeh EH-ta!*
wrong	неправильно	*n'yeh-PRA-veel-na*

DICTIONARY

X-ray	рентген	*r' yent-GHEN*

year	год	*goht*
yellow	жёлтый	*ZH'YOL-tee*
yes	да	*da*
yesterday	вчера	*f cheh-RA*
yet	ещё	*yesh-CHO*
you (sing. familiar)	ты	*twee*
you (pl.) (also sing. formal)	вы	*vwee*
young	молодой	*ma-la-DOY*
your	ваш	*vahsh*

zero	ноль	*nohl'*
zipper	молния	*MOHL-nee-ya*
zone	зона	*ZO-na*
zoo	зоопарк	*zo-oh-PARK*